ABOUT THE
STARMONT READER'S GUIDES TO CONTEMPORARY
SCIENCE FICTION AND FANTASY AUTHORS

The past two decades have seen an enormous upsurge in the interest in science fiction and fantasy. It is rare to find a bookstore that doesn't now prominently feature brightly colored examples of space and magic. It is unusual to find a high school, college, or university that doesn't offer at least one science fiction or fantasy course. Most significantly, it is becoming increasingly difficult to meet someone who hasn't succumbed to the lure of these two entertaining literatures. The Starmont Reader's Guides were created to satisfy the needs and interests of this varied readership. Bringing together acknowledged authorities, the series offers a thorough examination of each author; indeed, many of these efforts represent the first time the authors have been examined in book form. Each volume is divided into a chronological table of the author's life and literary career, a full biography, chapters on the major works or groups of works, and both primary and secondary bibliographies. Without sacrificing the sophistication that each author creates in his or her fiction, they clearly and cogently explore and explain the important issues, providing depth and understanding for both the beginning and the sophisticated reader.

It is hoped that the Starmont Reader's Guides will be of value to the student, teacher, librarian, scholar and fan by contributing to our understanding of the many authors and fascinating works that have provided us all with so much pleasure and insight.

Dr. Roger C. Schlobin, Series Editor
Department of English
Purdue University, North Central Campus

MARION
ZIMMER BRADLEY

Starmont Reader's Guide 27
ISSN 0272-7730

ROSEMARIE ARBUR

Series Editor: Roger C. Schlobin

R. Reginald

the Borgo Press

San Bernardino, California
MCMLXXXVI

For Willie,
'cause this one makes four

Library of Congress Cataloging in Publication Data:

Arbur, Rosemarie.
  Marion Zimmer Bradley.

  (Starmont reader's guide ; 27)
  Includes bibliographies and index.
  1. Bradley, Marion Zimmer--Criticism and interpretation.
  2. Science fiction, American--History and criticism.
  I. Title.   II. Series.
  PS3552.R228Z55 1985   813'.54   85-2721
  ISBN 0-916732-96-7 (cloth, $15.95)
  ISBN 0-916732-95-9 (paper, $7.95)

Published by Starmont House, Inc., P.O. Box 851, Mercer Island, WA 98040, USA. Composition by The Borgo Press, San
Bernardino, CA. Cover design by Stephen E. Fabian.

First Edition---August, 1985

CONTENTS

ABOUT THE AUTHOR

ROSEMARIE ARBUR joined the faculty of Lehigh University (Bethlehem PA) in 1972; currently she is associate professor of English. The author of <u>Leigh Brackett, Marion Zimmer Bradley, Anne McCaffrey:</u> A <u>Primary</u> and <u>Secondary Bibliography</u>, she has contributed essays about science fiction to a variety of reference works, books, and journals. Her other publications include articles on literary theory, American and British romanticism, the teaching of writing, and a booklet on computer-assisted preparation of texts.

Besides teaching courses in American literature and literary theory, Arbur regularly teaches "Literature of Women," in which she employs some fantasy and science-fiction readings to achieve a "distance" from which her students can more comfortably make inferences about the status of women in contemporary culture. She also teaches the regular science-fiction course and has offered special courses about nonhuman characters, the literature of a technocracy, "Golden Age SF," and the novels of Ursula K. Le Guin and C. J. Cherryh.

PREFACE AND ACKNOWLEDGMENTS

This book is intended as a guide for those who want to know about the science fiction written by Marion Zimmer Bradley. It is not written for people who have written doctoral dissertations about science fiction nor for those who are about to, although both these groups may find here some fact, insight, or other valuable thing not found elsewhere. This book is what the title says: a reader's guide. As I put it together, I followed the general format of all the other books in this series, so there are a chronology, an introductory chapter, two comprehensive bibliographies, and an index.

I wrote this book with the General Reader in mind. If you are reading this, you qualify. You've heard of Bradley's science fiction and want to know a bit more than you do at present. You've read some books or stories that Marion Zimmer Bradley wrote and learned that she's the author of a group of science-fiction books about the planet Darkover; if you want to read about that planet but do not know quite where to begin, this book will help. You've read, perhaps, a Darkover novel or two and wonder how the different works that make up the Darkover "series" relate to one another or make up some whole. Here you will find facts presented as accurately as possible, and here you will find comments on Bradley's science fiction that, I hope, will lead to clarification.

When I first began to teach literature courses—before I got to teaching seminars in literary criticism to graduate students—my most important self-imposed commandment was "Don't make them hate to read it." That still holds true. I hope this book can help make reading Bradley's fiction more fun and more rewarding (because I hope it helps make what Bradley's done a little more familiar). In any case, I hope I've set things up for the success of _readers_: in case I fail, my readers have to go to Bradley; and, in case of my complete success, they go to Bradley's works with information and enthusiasm.

* * * * *

The dedication is unusual. Since he is not a tall dog, just a large and substantial one, Willie must be credited with "underseeing" and supporting, usually from a position on the floor with his sturdy back aligned firmly against the back legs of my chair. At times he made it difficult for me to escape this task; at other times, impossible. And, since he is an old fellow now, it is altogether suitable for me to acknowledge formally the important role this pedigreed son of a yellow Lab bitch and her equally purebred German Shepherd paramour has had in sustaining the writing efforts that have taken his humans away from long walks and other more pleasant things. I make this acknowledgment seriously, for this is the fourth monstrous package of words that Willie has underseen; the others were two doctoral dissertations and one bibliographical volume devoted to three separate authors. He may not be A.K.C., but just his support of the two Ph.D. theses must rank at least comparably with a Utility Dog championship.

Then there are inanimate entities to be reckoned with. They cannot act, but if this book is an event, then they are at least important instrumental causes. Were it not for the help of the Lehigh University Computing Center's DEC 20, my TeleVideo terminal, and the Racal-Vadic modem that connects me electromagnetically to the big computer, this book would be a mess of typewritten pages strewn on the floor of my study awaiting a final agonizing job of typing. Were it not for LUCC's version of Unilogic's Scribe, I might, if I were very lucky and over-motivated, be thinking about getting ready to make an index sometime later on. I cannot thank these unwitting and unmindful entities, and I do not; I merely acknowledge their utility, and, if they could truly know, they'd reckon this mention of their being used as fair enough.

And then there are the human persons without whose help this book would surely never have attained its present form. By mentioning the Science Fiction Research Association, I can implicitly thank those people whose names do not appear here because of accidental lapses of my memory, but, in a very important sense, the SFRA itself deserves and has my deepest thanks. When most other motivations left me, I could not forget my responsibility to "science-fiction people," and by that term I mean not only the professors and other sorts who take science fiction seriously but also the writers I have met at the Association's yearly conferences. The SFRA is a true academic community, a collection of readers, writers, critics, agents, editors, and teachers who are mutually supportive. As I've remembered that, I've had to return to my desk-chair and get on with my share of the work.

As for individual persons, they are too numerous to list with accuracy and too worthy of my gratitude to discuss as "those who helped." So, because they found me copies of works I could not find, loaned me typescripts of novels not yet printed, said things that I realized later were take-off points for my own thoughts, or helped in other ways, I say "thank you" here by this brief mention: Don and Elsie Wollheim; Nora Wainer; David Hartwell; Lisa Waters; Jacqueline Lichtenberg; Mary T. Brizzi; Tom Whitehead of Temple University; Mary Jo Walker; Joe Goldstein and Tom Dinsmore of Lehigh University's Office of Research; Roger Schlobin, my always-patient editor; and Steve Maier, my **bredu** and husband.

I save for last the human Necessary Cause, the one who is, rather obviously, Marion Zimmer Bradley. She wrote the novels and stories that this book is all about. Not only did she write them in the sense of causing them to be, however; she wrote them in the very special way that makes a serious consideration of her contributions to science-fiction literature a necessity in a critical series with the scope that this one has. Marion has been generous in her gifts of time to this endeavor. When I was compiling the primary and secondary bibliographies, she invited me into her home and set before me, for several days, table-tops-full of her own copies of her writings. During that time, she let me borrow overnight some of the science fiction she had written and that had long been out of print and impossible to find and read elsewhere. And, even though she was writing--one morning she had completed twenty pages of a novel before I arrived at her door at nine o'clock--she frequently took time to explain the publishing history of this or that work, and more frequently simply talked. From these conversations and from the correspondence we've had since that time, I've learned a great deal not just about her and her works but about the science-fiction community as well. I am grateful. I speak for many--and for many reasons--when I set down here the understated "Thank you, MZB."

I

CANON AND CHRONOLOGY

1930   Born (3 June) in East Greenbush, New York, a small
        farming community near Albany and the foothills of
        the Adirondack Mountains, to Evelyn Parkhurst
        Conklin and Leslie Raymond Zimmer.

1936   Does not begin school because she is physically too
        little to walk a mile through snow-drifts to and
        from the school-bus stop. Does, however, perform
        her share of the family's farm chores.

1937   Begins elementary education in September at the
        East Schodack School. Skips two grades before
        junior high school.

1940   Has read the Sidney Lanier edition of the Arthurian
        legends (a gift from her maternal grandfather) so
        thoroughly that she knows the story virtually by
        heart.

1941   Begins seventh grade at East Greenbush, New York,
        school.

1943   Begins tenth grade at Columbia High School (in East
        Greenbush).

1944   Begins to write a novel set in Britain during the
        time of the Romans; eventually it influences
        The Mists of Avalon (1983).

1944-45 Plays hooky regularly but creatively: instead of
        being in school, she goes to the library of the New
        York State Department of Education. There she
        reads the entire ten volumes of The Golden Bough

and fifteen volumes of a reference work on comparative religions.

1945   Outlines the fantasy-novel that later becomes The Sword of Aldones; the concept of Darkover begins to form.

1946   At the end of her junior year, realizes that she has sufficient academic credit to enter New York State College for Teachers and is graduated from Columbia High School in June. Begins college in Albany, New York, in September. Finishes writing The King and the Sword, never to be published; its seven families of telepaths develop the concept of Darkover further.

1947   Is bedridden with rheumatic fever in spring after nursing her family through scarlet fever during the winter.

         Meets Dorothy Quinn, with whom she shared the first drafts of Web of Darkness, Web of Light; edits her own fanzine, Astra's Tower. In the fall, attends her first science-fiction ("Fan-vets") conference in New York City.

1948   With friends, organizes a very small conference in the spring.

1948-49   Writes a long fantasy called Web of Darkness, Web of Light which, after at least four re-writings and much polishing, becomes Web of Light and Web of Darkness, published by Pocket Books in 1983.

1949   "Stops out" of college in February. Marries Robert A. Bradley, who shares her interest in science fiction, in October. Moves to Texas, where her husband is employed by the railroad. Wins science-fiction story contest; the story was reprinted in the fanzine column of Amazing.

1950   First son, David Stephen Bradley, born in Albany,

New York (18 November).

1953   First published science-fiction stories, "Women Only" and "Keyhole," appear in _Vortex_.

1954   "Centaurus Changeling" appears in _The Magazine of Fantasy and Science Fiction_, and her professional career begins in earnest. Other science fiction: "Year of the Big Thaw," "Falcons of Narabedla" (serialized in a fanzine, _Dimensions_, ed. Harlan Ellison), "Jackie Sees a Star," and "The Crime Therapist."

1955   "The Climbing Wave" (in _F&SF_) and "Exiles of Tomorrow" are published.

1956   "Death Between the Stars," "Peace in the Wilderness," and "Naughty Venusianne" (the last a double pseudonymous collaboration with Forrest J Ackerman) appear.

        A SouthwestCon in Dallas is the first science-fiction fan gathering she's attended since 1948.

1957   "Bird of Prey" is published. Begins professional correspondence with Donald A. Wollheim, then science-fiction editor at Ace Books. Later in the year, meets Wollheim in person at Dallas. Correspondence continues as Wollheim buys _The Door Through Space_ and, later, _Falcons of Narabedla_ (1964).

1958   "The Stars are Waiting," "Collector's Item," and "The Planet Savers" are published.

1959   "The Wind People," "A Dozen of Everything," "To Err is Inhuman," and "Conquering Hero" are published.

1960   "The Wild One" and "Seven From the Stars" appear.

1961   Her first science-fiction novel, _The Door Through Space_, appears as an Ace double; it is an expansion of "Bird of Prey" (1957). Wollheim buys The Planet Savers and The Sword of Aldones. Bradley resumes her college education at Hardin-Simmons University in the fall. To finance her education, she begins to publish stories and novels of the "romantic" subgenre, somewhat analogous to the "Harlequin Romances" of the present. "Mama, Don't Let Him Have My Babies!" (printed with no author's name) appears in True Experience.

1962   A critical year: Seven From the Stars, The Sword of Aldones, and The Planet Savers appear as Ace doubles, the latter two in the same volume. "A Meeting in the Hyades" appears in a fanzine, Anduril; "Treason of the Blood" in Web Terror Stories; and Amazing publishes "Black and White" and "Measureless to Man." In addition, two Monarch romance-novels and two "true-confessions"-type stories appear under pseudonyms of Lee Chapman and Miriam Gardner or no name at all.

Separates from Bradley and moves to Abilene, Texas, to continue college. Meets Walter Breen in June in New York City.

1963   The Sword of Aldones is nominated for a Hugo; it, Philip K. Dick's The Man in the High Castle, and H. Beam Piper's Little Fuzzy are too close to call before the final ballot. Bradley "campaigns" for Little Fuzzy, and The Man in the High Castle wins. The Colors of Space, ostensibly a "juvenile," appears. So do "Phoenix" (with Ted White), "Another Rib" (with Juanita Coulson), and two Monarch romance-novels (under pseudonyms of Miriam Gardner and Morgan Ives).

1964   The Bloody Sun, the central novel of Darkover, appears; The Dark Intruder and Other Stories and The Falcons of Narabedla make up an Ace double. One of the pseudonymous romances is revised and issued in Australia, as Morgan Ives, and a new one is published here, as Miriam Gardner.

Earns bachelor's degree at Hardin-Simmons, having majored in English, educational psychology, and Spanish literature. Leaves Abilene, Texas, for Berkeley, California; divorce ends marriage with Bradley. Marries Walter Breen; second son, Patrick Russell Breen, born (31 October). She, husband, and son live in Berkeley but spend summers in New York City.

1965   Star of Danger, another Darkover novel, appears; so does Castle Terror, a gothic. Two science-fiction stories written for the young adult market, "The Blue Strangers" and "Danger: Martian at Large," sold, though details of their actual publications remain unknown.

1966   No science fiction, but two pseudonymous romances are published. Earl Kemp, not Bradley, is responsible for the pornographic scene near the beginning of her Knives of Desire (Evening Readers/Corinth), written as Morgan Ives.

Daughter, Moira Evelyn Dorothy Breen, born in Berkeley (10 January).

Enrolls in graduate courses in counseling psychology at the University of California, Berkeley (had taken some graduate work in psychology during senior year at Hardin-Simmons).

She and Breen, with Diana Paxson, hold the first tournament of the Society for Creative Anachronism (SCA).

1967   Stops graduate work after spring term. Gothic, Souvenir of Monique (Evening Readers/Corinth), is published.

She and Breen hold second SCA tournament.

Family moves to New York (Staten Island) in August; remains there until 1972.

1968   Another gothic, <u>Bluebeard's Daughter</u>, appears.

She, Breen, and about fifteen friends in New York City area found the "East Kingdom" of the SCA.

1969   <u>The Brass Dragon</u>, a science fiction "juvenile," published.

1970   <u>The Winds of Darkover</u> appears as half of an Ace double. Its title is changed before publication from "The <u>Wings</u> of" because of a complication arising from the illustration for the cover.

1971   <u>The World Wreckers</u> appears. Its internal chronology makes it the final Darkover novel; it is a conscious attempt--doomed to failure--to finish off Darkover as a setting for her science fiction.

Donald A. Wollheim encourages her to write another Darkover novel for DAW Books.

1972   <u>Darkover Landfall</u> becomes the first of the DAW Darkover novels; Wollheim renamed it (from "Summer of the Ghost Wind").

Because one of its characters must carry an unwanted pregnancy to term, <u>Landfall</u> creates a serious controversy among feminist and other writers, readers, and fans.

Berkley publishes <u>Dark Satanic</u>, a gothic fantasy, and a small California press publishes <u>Witch Hill</u> under a new pseudonym, Valerie Graves. The Breens return to California, first renting in Oakland and Berkeley, then (November) moving into the home now called Greyhaven. No plans for any more relocations.

1973   DAW publishes <u>Hunters of the Red Moon</u>, a major science-fiction adventure novel. Bradley acknowledges her brother, Paul Edwin Zimmer, as the first writer of the novel's excellent fighting scenes.

Ace reprints Souvenir of Monique, and Tempo Books (NY) publishes In the Steps of the Master, a novelization of the Universal Television series The Sixth Sense.

Obtains an ordination certificate to be able, legally, to do psychological ("pastoral") counseling.

1974   DAW publishes The Spell Sword, a Darkover novel that relies on the same informal collaboration as Hunters of the Red Moon. The semi-professional publisher, T-K Graphics, releases The Jewel of Arwen and The Parting of Arwen. (The latter work was reprinted the following year under the pseudonym of Alfrida Rivers.)

1975   DAW releases The Heritage of Hastur, a long Darkover novel thought by many to be the best so far. Ace publishes Endless Voyage, an independent science-fiction novel about the long-lived explorers who travel through normal space to open new worlds to humankind. Tempo Books issues another novelization, this one of a TV Movie of the Week: Can Ellen Be Saved?

The Friends of Darkover, a fan group interested in Darkover and other alternate universes, forms and begins to publish the Darkover Newsletter.

1976   Another big year. "The Day of the Butterflies" is chosen for inclusion in The DAW Science Fiction Reader, a special anthology that celebrates DAW's publication of two hundred titles. Ace reprints The Planet Savers and The Sword of Aldones as separate volumes; in the former, "The Waterfall," a Darkover short story, is published for the first time. And Ballantine releases Drums of Darkness, a gothic fantasy.

The Shattered Chain, a long Darkover novel that focuses on the "Free Amazons" and Darkovan womanhood generally, is issued by DAW; critics of Darkover Landfall seem to have to do an about-face, for in this work the "heroine" requiring rescue is a Terran man. "Hero's Moon" is published in F&SF.

Puts ministerial certificate to use, counseling at the Pacific Center for Human Growth. Begins to consider further study in religion/counseling seriously.

1977   The "big-book-a-year" habit becomes established: DAW prints The Forbidden Tower, which subsequently is nominated for the Nebula Award and comes in second on the Hugo Award balloting. The Sword of Aldones, and The Heritage of Hastur are reprinted in permanent hardcover editions by Gregg Press (G.K. Hall & Company). Nor is short science-fiction neglected: "The Engine" and "A Genuine Old Master" appear.

The Friends of Darkover begin publication of a fanzine: Starstone #1 appears.

1978   A year for getting earlier works back in print: DAW reissues Hunters of the Red Moon, Ace reprints The World Wreckers, and Gregg Press puts out Darkover Landfall in hardcover. In Great Britain, Methuen reprints The Brass Dragon; The Bloody Sun, Darkover Landfall, The Shattered Chain, The Spell Sword, Star of Danger, and The Winds of Darkover are released by Arrow Books.

Stormqueen! becomes the latest Darkover novel (DAW Books), and The Ruins of Isis appears as a trade paperback.

Evidence of continuing interest in women on Darkover is evident in the Darkover fanzines: Darkover Newsletter #9-10 contains "Amazon Excerpt," "Amazon Fragment," and "Everything But

Freedom," while <u>Starstone</u> #1 features "The Keeper's Price" (with Lisa Waters) and "The Lesson of the Inn."

Receives the "Invisible Little Man Award" (designed to give due recognition to a science-fiction writer who has not won a Nebula or a Hugo Award).

1979   Receives the Hamilton-Brackett Memorial Award for <u>The</u> <u>Forbidden</u> <u>Tower</u>; new novels are <u>The</u> <u>Catch</u> <u>Trap</u> (hardcover, mainstream), <u>The</u> <u>Survivors</u> (sequel to <u>Hunters</u> <u>of</u> <u>the</u> <u>Red</u> <u>Moon</u> and written jointly with her brother Paul), and thoroughly revised versions of <u>The</u> <u>Bloody</u> <u>Sun</u> and <u>Endless</u> <u>Voyage</u> (now retitled <u>Endless</u> <u>Universe</u>). Bound with <u>The</u> <u>Bloody</u> <u>Sun</u> is a new Darkover story, "To Keep the Oath." "The Secret of the Blue Star" appears in Robert Lynn Asprin's experimental anthology, <u>Thieves'</u> <u>World</u>, and Bradley herself edits a small-press Darkover anthology, <u>Legends</u> <u>of</u> <u>Hastur</u> <u>and</u> <u>Cassilda</u>, which includes her own story, "The Legend of Lady Bruna."

In Great Britain, Arrow Books reprints <u>The</u> <u>Sword</u> <u>of</u> <u>Aldones</u>, while at home reprinting ventures continue. Ace reissues <u>The</u> <u>Door</u> <u>Through</u> <u>Space</u>, <u>Falcons</u> <u>of</u> <u>Narabedla</u>, and <u>Seven</u> <u>From</u> <u>the</u> <u>Stars</u>, and Pocket Books puts out <u>The</u> <u>Ruins</u> <u>of</u> <u>Isis</u> in mass-market form. Gregg Press completes its hardcover reprinting of the Darkover novels with <u>The</u> <u>Bloody</u> <u>Sun</u> (revised edition), <u>The</u> <u>Forbidden</u> <u>Tower</u>, <u>The</u> <u>Planet</u> <u>Savers</u> (without "The Waterfall"), <u>The</u> <u>Shattered</u> <u>Chair</u>, <u>The</u> <u>Spell</u> <u>Sword</u>, <u>Star</u> <u>of</u> <u>Danger</u>, <u>Stormqueen!</u>, <u>The</u> <u>Winds</u> <u>of</u> <u>Darkover</u>, and <u>The</u> <u>World</u> <u>Wreckers</u>.

Offsetting the retrospective effect of so much reprinting are Bradley's month at the New York Public Library and an even longer period of research in England, which will bear fruit in an Arthurian fantasy tentatively entitled "Mistress of Magic." Between these two research trips, Bradley is a well-received special guest at the June 1979

Science Fiction Research Association's annual
conference.

1980   The House Between the Worlds is published in
        hardcover by Doubleday in April and by the Science
        Fiction Book Club in August. Survey Ship comes out
        as an illustrated Ace trade paperback. Two to
        Conquer is the year's new DAW Darkover novel. DAW
        also publishes The Keeper's Price and Other
        Stories, the first commercial Darkover anthology,
        edited by Bradley and including her "Blood Will
        Tell," "The Hawk-Master's Son," and her and Lisa
        Waters' title story. "Elbow Room" appears in
        Stellar Science Fiction Stories #5, and "Excerpt--
        Thendara House" appears in another of Bradley's
        small-press Darkover anthologies, Tales of the Free
        Amazons.

        Ace continues to reprint: The Planet Savers and
        The Sword of Aldones with a non-fiction essay,
        "Darkover Retrospective," are released as one
        volume; others are The Brass Dragon, Star of
        Danger, The Winds of Darkover, and The World
        Wreckers.

        On the basis of her previously published science
        fiction, ranks fifth in Hugo "Grand Master of
        Fantasy (Gandalf) Award" voting.

        After several years of preparation and study, is
        ordained a priest in the Pre-Nicene Catholic
        Church; establishes the Centre for Nontraditional
        Religion and converts what was to be a studio
        apartment over her large garage into a meeting
        place for those groups that want and need one.

1981   Sharra's Exile is the DAW Darkover novel for the
        year, and a revised, expanded mass-market edition
        of The House Between the Worlds is released by Del
        Rey Books. Ace reissues Survey Ship in mass-market
        form.

18

The Centre for Nontraditional Religion becomes incorporated.

1982   Edits Sword of Chaos, an anthology of stories about Darkover that includes two of her own, "A Sword of Chaos" and "The Lesson of the Inn." Hawkmistress! is the DAW Darkover novel.

Knopf, having bought the "Mistress of Magic" manuscript, requests that Bradley lengthen it; it becomes The Mists of Avalon.

1983   Web of Light (to be followed by Web of Darkness) is published by Timescape after at least a year's delay because Donning/Starblaze had edited and rewritten so much of the original manuscript that Bradley took legal recourse to reclaim and resell it.
The Mists of Avalon (originally "Mistress of Magic") is published by Knopf in hardcover and immediately appears on the New York Times' bestseller list. Its sales and reviews indicate that it is certainly not just another Arthurian novel. The Colors of Space (revised and expanded edition) is issued by Donning/Starblaze as a trade paperback.

Bradley edits Greyhaven, an original anthology of fantasy that includes "The Incompetent Magician," a story that features the character Lythande of "The Secret of the Blue Star" from Thieves' World (1979).

Thendara House is the DAW Darkover novel, interestingly less autonomous than the others; about Magda and Jaelle of The Shattered Chain, this book is not only a sequel itself but suggests that a new "Free Amazons" Darkover novel will soon be forthcoming.

1984   Bradley has good reason to distrust Terran technology after her first word processor erased the disks that contained half a novel. Nevertheless, she shrewdly replaces that evil machine with a user-friendly DEC device. Thus City of Sorcery, the DAW Darkover novel, appears--with a cover by James Gurney that depicts a younger, taller, yet suspiciously familiar-looking "Darkovan" woman.

"Somebody Else's Magic" is the cover story in F&SF's 35th Anniversary issue: another tale about Lythande. Dyan Ardais' youth is the subject of "Oathbreaker," and further narratives--about Lythande and about Darkover--are ready for publication. Bradley also brings back two characters from Dark Satanic in The Inheritor (Tor Books), an occult fantasy set in presentday San Francisco.

The Mists of Avalon, already in Science Fiction Book Club hardcover is reprinted here as a trade paperback and in Great Britain as a mass-market (very thick) one. Her mainstream novel, The Catch Trap, gets a new cover for this year's release in paper.

And, with no lessening of her fictional output, Bradley takes on further editorial ventures. The DAW anthology Sword and Sorceress (women as wizards and warriors) appears in the spring; DAW will publish its sequel and the third Darkover anthology in 1985. So, not only does City of Sorcery conclude a trilogy set up by The Shattered Chain and Thendara House but Magda and Camilla could just be ready for a novel that truly ends their quest...if Bradley can give them some computer time! One is tempted to suspect that her deepening interest in magic will be vindicated as she proves that even her new word processor is no match for the stories she conjures so swiftly by mind.

II

BIOGRAPHICAL AND CRITICAL INTRODUCTION

Marion Zimmer Bradley has been writing science fiction for at least thirty-five years; she has had her work professionally published for thirty. Although she almost won a Hugo Award for The Sword of Aldones twenty years ago, only after the publication of The Heritage of Hastur in 1975 has she been widely recognized as a major science-fiction writer. The Heritage of Hastur is one of the more important novels in her Darkover series, and it has been followed, at the rate of about one book a year, with other works set on the planet Darkover. Her earliest published works were, as is usual for a beginning writer, short stories and novelettes. Although she has concentrated more on longer forms—even her novels have become noticeably longer as her career has developed—she continues to publish short stories with regularity. And, as if eighteen Darkover novels were not enough, Bradley has, while keeping to her one-Darkover-novel-a-year pattern, been writing and having published other works of science fiction and fantasy almost as frequently.

The delayed recognition of her stature has had two pleasant advantages. Readers "discovering" Marion Zimmer Bradley only recently have been able to find in the works of a "new" author excellences that send them back to the bookstore for more and, since Bradley seems to grow more prolific with each passing year, these readers have been able to find newly published works that do live up to their rather high expectations. The second advantage is that Bradley's works have become truly popular at just about the same time as she seems to have outgrown both temporal and aesthetic limitations. That is to say, Marion Zimmer Bradley seems always to have been able to write a well-plotted story, but recently, she seems to be able to write consistently good science fiction with nearly awesome frequency.

A quick glance at one recent year's output illustrates this point. In the fall of 1982, <u>Hawkmistress</u>!--a major Darkover novel--was published by DAW Books. By late January 1983, <u>Web of Light</u> was available as a Timescape paperback. (1) At nearly the same time, Knopf released her <u>Mists of Avalon</u> in hardcover; a second printing was necessary even before the first had reached the bookstores, and by March the novel was in its fifth printing. At present there are at least a hundred thousand hardcover copies in print. <u>The Mists of Avalon</u> is a long book, a powerful re-telling of Arthurian legend, and its several superlative attributes place it, according to one reviewer, "in the ranks of the major fantasies"; (2) it is one of the few that can endure comparison with Tolkien's <u>Rings</u> and Le Guin's <u>Earthsea</u> trilogies without seeming either trivial or derivative. Then, Donning/Starblaze issued the revised edition of <u>The Colors of Space</u>, DAW published <u>Greyhaven</u>, an original anthology of fantasy edited by Bradley, and in September both the mass-market reprint of <u>The Colors of Space</u> (Pocket Books) and the new Darkover novel <u>Thendara House</u> (DAW) appeared. The latter is the sequel to <u>The Shattered Chain</u> and the middle book of a "trilogy" (<u>City of Sorcery</u> is the present "conclusion") that explores in depth the life-options and problems of women on Darkover.

From another perspective, Bradley's delayed recognition brings with it two disadvantages. One is that many of her early and less excellent works have been reprinted, so that not <u>everything</u> one finds on bookstore shelves is uniformly good. The other is that new readers may experience some difficulty, after enjoying the most recent of Bradley's works, simply in finding time to locate and read the novels and stories she has had published in the past.

The critical and popular recognition Bradley has recently received introduces several significant attributes of her personality, her authorial persona, and her career as a science-fiction writer. (3) Like most serious readers of science fiction, Marion Zimmer found herself a self-decreed exile from the world of those mediocre romances and adventure stories that comprised the reading matter of her teen-aged contemporaries. By happy default, she became a science-fiction fan, and, as early as 1944, she began to write about her own "romances" and "adventures"--those which exis-

ted in the worlds engendered by her lively imagination. In
other words, Marion Zimmer Bradley has been a lifelong, in-
good-standing member of the science-fiction world.

"IN PROPRIA PERSONA"—OR THE REVERSE

Discussing the content of literary works, critics often
use the phrase in propria persona to identify passages of
thematic importance which seem to be authorial intrusions or
comments written "in (the writer's) own person." Sometimes
these passages identify themselves by a shift in point of
view, as if the writer were commenting upon the incidents
and characters that are otherwise "just being told about,"
that are the self-evident reasons for the narration. In
other instances, it is the critic or reader who identifies
such passages. Since the turn of the century, when Henry
James's works concentrated on a single source of narration
for an entire novel and could rather easily be viewed as
alternating "scenes" and "summaries," consistency of narration has become a nearly universal rule.

When the rule appears to be broken (when there is more
than one narrator, when the narrator presents "summary" that
is overlong when compared with "scene" (direct action and
dialogue) or when the narrator seems to be telling the story
"inconsistently" by implying more than a single attitude
about what is transpiring in the novel), the prevalent
critical activities have been first to detect the plurality
of attitudes and second to determine which of them embodies
the author's personal judgments and which belong appropriately to the ever-consistent narrative voice. The danger
inherent in this critical activity is that the readers may
find themselves exercising their imaginations or employing
their critical acuities instead of following the narration
that is the novel. The danger is insidious, moreover,
because readers invariably find something of thematic nature
with which they agree, disagree, or at the least connect
with some ideology or "ism"; and it is only natural to
wonder if one's own set of personal beliefs is reflected by
the author of the literary work one is reading.

One approach to this matter of the reader's own and

some author's personal set of values is to regard every work
of literature as originating in some person's (the writer's)
head, but to regard every work as being transmitted by means
chosen consciously or unconsciously by the writer. That is
to say: there is a person who lives in Berkeley, who writes
science fiction, and whose name is Marion Zimmer Bradley.
When this person writes (tells a story), she has by the time
the words are appearing on paper "chosen" or "created" a
voice she deems the most efficacious one to tell the story
the way she wants it to be told. Generally, by sitting at
her typewriter prepared to write a narrative, this woman has
adopted a set of attitudes--a persona--with the qualities
needed to produce a work of literature: she has adopted,
created, or projected the persona of "author." As she
concentrates further on what she wants her literary work to
be, this writer refines the authorial persona to be this or
that kind of narrator (if the work is, as it is usually, a
story). The narrative persona may differ from book to book,
and even within a book (there are two narrators of The
Heritage of Hastur, for instance), but the authorial persona
usually retains certain identifying characteristics, no
matter what the precise qualities of various novels and
stories may be. To avoid confusion, "Marion Zimmer Bradley"
(or "Bradley") is used hereafter to designate the woman who
lives in Berkeley, while "MZB" designates that set of attitudes and other attributes--the authorial persona--which is
the intermediary between the woman who writes and the narratives we read. This distinction is critical to an understanding of her work.

One quality bestowed upon Bradley's authorial persona
is, by virtue of a long career and the knowledge that "the
story" is important, a real virtuosity and competence in the
making of a plot. With Two to Conquer, for example, innocent readers find themselves caught up in the characters and
incidents of the novel only to realize that there are merely
twenty pages left to read: "However will she manage to
resolve these conflicts in only twenty pages?" By the time
that readers finish the novel, the conflicts are resolved--
not by any contrivance but by resolving only the conflicts
that the novel itself developed. That is, the wars and
feuds of the "hundred kingdoms" continue, compliance with
Varzil's Compact remains in doubt, but the fortunes of Bard

di Asturien—the protagonist of the novel—are by the end satisfyingly certain. The real plot of the novel is convincingly resolved.

Another characteristic of Bradley's authorial persona is an interest in the actualities and potentialities of women. To anyone even somewhat familiar with her work, it is clear that a significant part of what Bradley writes is "women's science fiction." It is easy to assume, on the basis of her strong feminine charcterizations, that her personal beliefs as well as her authorial stances are feminist. Any such assumptions are wrong. Deriving as it does from a multifaceted and independent personality, Bradley's habitual authorial stance is the combination of personal attributes that will best get the story told.

It is particularly important to remember the distinction between person and persona when one deals with Bradley's "works about women." The woman writing the story may as likely as not have projected an authorial persona whose orientation is about one hundred and eighty degrees different from her personal beliefs. Marion Zimmer Bradley makes no excuses for her aversion to Tiptree's "Houston, Houston, Do You Read?" Her personal feeling is that Tiptree's elimination of the male half of the human species in the novella is at best an unhealthy manifestation. Were Bradley to adopt the persona of "literary critic," however, it is likely that she would find in Tiptree's structuring of the plot and delineation of incident and character some praiseworthy literary attributes.

Yet Bradley is essentially a writer, not a critic, and her own Ruins of Isis is evidence that she can project and sustain an authorial persona that is at least sympathetic to separatist feminism. One cannot read Ruins without feeling some sympathy for Cendri, a young woman who lets her marriage interrupt her own academic progress so that her new husband's may be furthered. The Ruins of Isis presents Cendri's justified feelings of bitterness—for her husband, Dal, must play the housepet role and then, it seems, must displace his hostility at the "woman's world" of Isis onto his wife by over-aggressive sexual contact. The novel also presents the kind of common-sense division of labor according to sex (men have the muscles and the more acute sex drives; let men do the heavy work without forcing on them

prolonged and tedious occupations) in a way that, while
ironic, is just a bit too sympathetic to be dismissed as
parody. There is some psycho-physiological basis for the
cliche of women's "putting up with" their husbands' and
lovers' anxiety-related need for the sexual act, just as
some men in contemporary culture undoubtedly relish at least
the idea of being "one of the boys" who enjoy the all-male
camaraderie of the hunting or fishing vacation. (4)

If one is to read The Ruins of Isis with sensitivity,
one has to recognize the separatist-feminist aspect of the
authorial voice. The novel is not a simple one, although it
appears to do a gender-role reversal in the interests of a
feminist theme. The novel displays as well the vulnerabi-
lity of men who must be "all man" and never display (except
in religious ritual) the "gentler emotions," to the end that
"men are humans, too" is a significant part of the work's
thematic statements. If readers recognize the irony of the
social conditions that prevail on Isis, they are interpre-
ting one theme as "women, too, are human beings." And they
are correct: The Ruins of Isis is more about the oppression
of women than it is about the hypothetical oppression of men
in a women's society, and it is able to keep this thematic
focus because its author is able to control the attitudes
expressed by the persona who tells the story.

That a woman who writes books finds the fictional
disappearance of men in one narrative unhealthy and yet in a
novel of her own reduces men to little more than draft
animals and sexual playthings is not, obviously, impossible.
Neither is it difficult to understand if one recognizes the
efficacy of various kinds of "author" in various kinds of
literary works. Bradley is not a feminist. Yet Bradley's
Ruins of Isis is without question polemical, and it is
polemical because of Bradley's choice of authorial persona.
To speak of the woman who lives in Berkeley and of The Ruins
of Isis, without floundering in contradictions, one needs
only to realize that this novel is transmitted by very
nearly the opposite of a persona that reflects with accuracy
the feelings and beliefs of its source. In other words,
Bradley can write in propria persona and, when she wishes,
in its reverse.

Thus, whatever Bradley herself thinks and feels about
feminism is--by the time it has been trasmuted during the

26

course of the creative, artistic process--both inaccessible from and irrelevant to the particular fictive work one has at hand. Her Darkover Landfall (1972) was reviled by feminist critics who felt strongly that the fictional refusal of an abortion to one of the chief women characters was symbolically or metaphorically or even literally a denunciation of a woman's right to choose to terminate an unwanted pregnancy. It is said that Joanna Russ's We Who Are About To... was a response to Bradley's novel, for Russ's feminine protagonist, marooned on an off-the-space-lanes world with several other characters, not only refuses to become pregnant but commits suicide rather than attempt to make a "lost colony" out of too few survivors of an accident.

Yet if one reads Bradley's Shattered Chain (1976) without knowing of the furor ignited by the earlier novel, one has to see in Kindra, Jaelle, Magda, and even the Lady Rohana fictional variations on the theme of women's right to self-determination. Darkover Landfall may or may not contain thematically misogynist "statements," but there is little doubt that The Shattered Chain is a feminist science-fiction novel. In fact, The Shattered Chain is one of the most thorough and sensitive science-fiction explorations of the variety of options available to a self-actualising woman; not only does it present us with four strong and different feminine characters who make crucial decisions about their lives but its depth of characterization permits us to examine in detail the consequences of these decisions.

Because the setting and mode of the novel are science fictional rather than mundane or "realistic," the variables affecting acts of choice may be simplified to the degree that they are thematically intelligible as well as credible. Set far in the future on a distant planet, the novel is the sort of thought-experiment that Ursula K. Le Guin discusses in her introduction to The Left Hand of Darkness. (5) Readers who might be put off by a society of separatist feminists in a verisimilar novel set in the here-and-now cannot feel the same way toward the Free Amazons who inhabit a world not only fictional but entirely hypothetical. And thus Bradley's novel is able credibly to present several women heroes (not "heroines") and cause its readers to ponder--at least subconsciously--the real analogues of these characters' science-fictional situations.

What these two novels tell us about Marion Zimmer Bradley is important, but it has little to do with her personal or authorial sexual politics. These novels tell us that the person who wrote them is an accomplished writer, able at will to project authorial personae that might, if they were personalities instead of crafted pre-literary creations, preclude the existence of one another. These novels show us that primary to the person who wrote them are the stories being told and the characters called into existence by their creation. Readers happy to see Jaelle fall in love with Peter Haldane and readers deeply disturbed that this emotional attachment threatens Jaelle's integrity as a Free Amazon are likely to be equally surprised that Bradley--the person, not the author--is unconcerned because she knows that "Jaelle will dump that turkey soon enough." (6) Similarly, readers who familiarize themselves with the culture of the Darkovans and sympathize with its values--who do these things largely because of how Bradley has presented Darkover--may be shocked to learn that, looking upon her Darkover novels as verbal artifacts, Marion Zimmer Bradley is secretly supportive of the mores of the Terran Empire. By personal choice, Bradley is a "city person"; were her sympathies truly pre-industrial or Darkovan, she could live a Darkovan sort of life in the hills above Berkeley or move even farther east to reside among the foothills of the Sierras. But because she is aware and appreciative of what current technology can make possible, she resides in a normal twentieth-century house, drives a car, uses state-of-the-art stereo to listen to opera and other classical music, and makes frequent trips across the bay to avail herself of the cultural advantages of San Francisco. These very different novels and very different attitudes illustrate the fact that Marion Zimmer Bradley and the fictions written by her are separate entities. That the novels exist in their own right and that they do not need to be explained by referring to the private life of their author tell us simply that their author is accomplished at her craft.

THE GIRL IS MOTHER TO...

Although every relevant fact about Bradley's life appears in the "Canon and Chronology," this addition of a few details in basically narrative form helps readers see Bradley's life as more than just a series of dates and events. First, a caveat: though correspondence between her actual experiences and some of the incidents she writes of may be interesting, the experience does not necessarily cause the fictional incident. And when Bradley is quoted as having said this or that about "what she meant," she is not necessarily revealing an intention. Most authors are reluctant to speak about what happens when they write, often because they do not consciously know and prefer to leave their unconscious minds unhampered by analytic probing. Bradley is among the contemporary few who can speak about what she is writing without having the story or novel seriously damaged by "talking it" before she writes. Still, it is prudent to think of such statements as "stated intentions" instead of actual ones, just as it is wise to recognize that experience in writing fiction is excellent preparation for speaking it. Duly warned, readers may still find information about Bradley's "real life" interesting and may draw cautious inferences from it. At least one such inference is this: after nearly forty years in the science-fiction world, the increasing successes of her Darkover novels and the wide recognition that The Mists of Avalon has brought her are not just good fortune but rewards that she truly deserves.

Marion Zimmer grew up on a farm during the Great Depression and the anxious years of World War II. Since the time she was able to lift an egg basket, she was assigned an increasing number of farm chores, and she did them. During the war, in fact, when her father was employed at Port of Albany doing salvage work, she and her brother Leslie virtually ran the family farm by themselves. Earlier in her childhood, Marion Zimmer probably contracted sub-clinical or undiagnosed rheumatic fever, or it may be that her having nursed her entire family through a winter of scarlet fever caused the rheumatic fever that kept her bedridden for months before her seventeenth birthday. Whatever the cause, Bradley has been subject to an atypical kind of arthritis, the symptoms of which vary with climate. To avoid the symptoms--which were severe in her late teens while she was living near Albany, and again when she and her family lived year-round on Staten island--she must simply "avoid cold, fatigue, and stress." (7) The relatively mild winters in Berkeley enable her to follow one third of that medical advice; the active life of a professional writer with a family to care for and other interests to follow makes it impossible for her--or anyone--to fill the second and third parts of the "prescription."

One might surmise that her probable illness during early childhood directed Marion Zimmer toward intellectual rather than athletic pursuits, and one could be correct. Nevertheless, the normal activities required of a child whose parents were farmers can hardly permit anyone to think of young Marion as frail. The delay of her formal education was the result, rather, of the inability of a relatively short child to walk, unattended, the miles between her home and the local school, especially when it was more likely than not--from November through February--that she would encounter deep snowdrifts on her way. (Even now, school-children in upstate New York can expect a special extended holiday--"mudweek"--when the first warm weather of the year does its work on a winter's accumulation of snow.)

Although she began first grade when she was seven instead of six, Marion Zimmer's academic progress enabled her to "skip" several grades in elementary school and, after taking more than the usual number of courses each year in high school, to be graduated only three weeks after her sixteenth birthday. The physical isolation of her home and the social dislocation caused by grade-skipping and heavier-than-usual academic workloads helped to mold Marion Zimmer into the category of "bright students" and to make her adolescence a relatively lonely one.

She was just the sort of young person for whom science fiction would have a special appeal. Having already read much (especially when she sneaked off to the New York Department of Education Library instead of attending classes), and having already written fantasy "novels" of her own,

Marion Zimmer's discovery of Startling Stories in August of 1946 proved to be a catalyst. Within a year, she attended a "Con" (short for science-fiction convention, a term widely used among science-fiction fans), and then began to edit a fanzine (a science-fiction fan's amateur magazine). Within two years, she and her friends organized and held a very small "Con" of their own.

From September of 1946 through February of 1949, Marion Zimmer attended the New York State College for Teachers, Albany (it has since become part of the state-wide university system: State University of New York at Albany). In October 1949, she married Robert A. Bradley, a man considerably older than she and also deeply interested in science fiction. He worked as a railroad telegrapher in Levelland, Texas, and it might be said that Marion Zimmer left her family's home near the Darkovan Hellers to take up residence among the Darkovan Dry Towns. She returned to Albany to bear her first child in 1950 and then went back to Texas and moved from Levelland to Tahoka, where her husband's transfer sent them. Tahoka had a population of about five thousand, but the next job-transfer--to Rochester, Texas, with a population of only 650--caused what amounted to "culture shock." The town, Bradley is fond of saying, consisted of a railroad station, cotton gin, gas station, school, Post Office and general store, and nine churches. Whatever orthodox Christian beliefs she may have had before, her allegiance to Christianity and interest in religion generally was soon suppressed by the narrow-minded sectarianism of her new hometown. As if by compensation, the warm, dry climate alleviated her arthritis, and the annual dust-storms frequently caused the sun to appear as a red disk hanging in a darkened sky. Add to this image the eerie color that is generated by tornado weather, and the guess that the "bloody sun" of Darkover was almost a reality in Texas cannot be too far off the mark.

As the decade of the fifties passed, the Bradleys' marriage lost its vitality. Hardin-Simmons University was in Abilene; early in 1962, the Bradleys separated, and Marion moved to Abilene to continue her college education. Her son accompanied her by choice, and she found herself in the unenviable situation of being simultaneously mother, student, homemaker, science-fiction writer, and formulaic-romance writer, the checks for which she and her son sorely needed.

In June of 1962, Bradley met Walter Breen in New York City. Eventually it was evident to them both that they wanted to marry and have children, but distance, Marion Bradley's unfinished education, and especially Robert Bradley's reluctance to divorce required them to wait. After the fall of 1963 school term, Marion was graduated from Hardin-Simmons with a triple major: English, educational psychology, and Spanish literature. Before she earned her bachelor's degree, she enrolled in several graduate-level courses in psychology. When she was graduated after the fall semester, she moved to Berkeley, where Breen was living, and early in 1964, she convinced Robert Bradley to grant the divorce that enabled her and Breen to marry almost immediately.

They did, and Patrick Russell Breen was born in Berkeley on 31 October. Only fourteen months later, on 10 January 1966, Moira Evelyn Dorothy Breen was born, also in Berkeley. A year and a half later, the Breens decided to remain in New York City—they had been spending their summers there since they were married—and in August of 1967 they made Staten Island their year-round home.

Despite the sense of achievement her continuing and then completing college brought her, and however emotionally satisfying and promising her second marriage was, Marion Bradley-then-Breen experienced some truly hard times. Marion Zimmer Bradley—she kept the name since she had already established herself as a science-fiction writer— found little material consolation during the latter years of her first marriage and the early ones of her second. She had been, since about 1959, writing Monarch Books romances for the money, initially to finance her education, then to support her and her first son while she was finishing college, and then, when Walter Breen was ill, to keep the household at least somewhat financially solvent. After what must have been a sorely wrenching time—with her husband's ill health, and their children, and her career as a science-fiction writer all making simultaneous and absolute demands on her—Marion Zimmer Bradley Breen was able, once the family was settled in Staten Island, to stop writing those formulaic and pseudonymous romances.

32

But the decade past seemed to have taken its toll, for Marion Zimmer Bradley seemed somehow to have lost her "sense of wonder": the science fiction she wanted to write evidently did not want to be written. The books she had written for the money gave her the opportunity to develop the discipline necessary for her craft and also to master the art of plotting a narrative, but they may have cost something of Bradley's native imaginative enthusiasm. The Brass Dragon, a young-adult novel published in 1969, is the only "new" piece of science fiction Bradley wrote during this period, and its dedication to her son David, "who saw the Brass Dragon in Texas," suggests that the story really belongs to the author's past. Even though The Winds of Darkover (1970) introduces Melitta Storn as one of the early women protagonists in science fiction, Bradley felt Darkover somehow receding from her.

The dedication of The World Wreckers (1971)--a novel that tries unsuccessfully to end the entire Darkover "experiment"--lists Anne McCaffrey, Juanita Coulson, Ursula Le Guin, and Randall Garrett as people who "kept (her) sense of wonder alive." (8) Coulson and Garrett were old friends, and the listing of McCaffrey and Le Guin calls to mind one of those pivotal experiences in Bradley's career. (9) At a science-fiction convention, Bradley was conversing with McCaffrey and mentioned the frustration she was experiencing--the loss of her sense of wonder and apparent inability to get into words what she wanted to write about. McCaffrey's response was to give Bradley a copy of Le Guin's recently published Left Hand of Darkness with the suggestion that reading it would work a psychological "cure." Evidently it did, as the dedication of The World Wreckers and the mention of a planet already named Winter in The Shattered Chain indicate.

In addition, Bradley notes that her relationship with Donald Wollheim evolved from a strictly professional one to a real friendship in 1971 or thereabouts. (10) Wollheim encouraged her to write another Darkover novel for his new publishing firm, DAW Books; Bradley did, and gave him Summer of the Ghost Wind which Wollheim, in the interest of marketing the novel, retitled Darkover Landfall. With her sense of wonder restored and an editor-friend's encouragement, Bradley began to write science fiction regularly and well.

From the early seventies, she has been producing an almost unbelievable number of novels about Darkover and about the universe identified by the presence of "The Unity," still others with entirely independent settings, and a healthy number of short stories. To borrow a metaphor from one of Anne McCaffrey's works, Marion Zimmer Bradley "bridled Pegasus" and has sat her mount quite steadily ever since. (11)

THE SCIENCE-FICTION WRITER

Like almost every professional writer, Marion Zimmer Bradley _must_ writes for two reasons. First, there is the absolute necessity, embedded deep within the personality, to put "it" into words. There are several descriptive labels for this quality. One, deriving from educational psychology, is "the need to achieve." Far from being a sign of some pathological condition--as the "need to drink" and the "need to overwork" may be for alcoholics and people whose lives are consumed by their occupations--the need to achieve is as natural for some people as the need to obey is for those dogs who eventually become obedience champions: it is simply a matter of personality. The people whose "achieving" takes the form of written and verbal expression are the people we call "writers."

Another set of labels is more likely to be misinterpreted, for if one speaks of another's "obsession" or "compulsion," one may be describing some personality dysfunction. Yet, as many psychologists and psychiatrists have remarked in all seriousness, "if there weren't obsessive-compulsive people around, nothing would ever get done." In this descriptive sense, we may speak of Bradley as one of those persons who becomes "obsessed" by an idea and then "compelled" to get the idea out of her head and onto paper as fully and as accurately as possible. If her personality were different from what it is, she would not be a writer; instead, she might satisfy her obsessions by fantasizing privately and at length about them, and we would never know that a temporary "preoccupation"--that time spent fantasizing--has deprived us of the opportunity to read a good story or novel.

Then there is the Freudian interpretation of those two terms. If we believe wholeheartedly in Freud, the "obsessive-compulsive" personality is an unhealthy one, fixated on the object of its obsession and unaware of the "real world" while some personality defect forces the person's consciousness to dwell upon whatever it is compelled to dwell upon. According to Freud, such a condition must arise from some pathology, and any writing or other achievement must be regarded as a symptom of whatever is wrong. Contemporary ego-psychology, however, disagrees with Freud: the artistic result of an obsessive-compulsive's musings need not be a symptom, or a sign that something is wrong, for it may simply be evidence that the artist has harnessed "neutral" psychic energies to produce a literary artwork.

Applied to Marion Zimmer Bradley, each of these labels or interpretations has some relevance. No one is so mentally healthy that some outlet isn't at times needed to stabilize emotions or "displace hostility" safely: one need only look at the numerous works of science fiction that are transparent attacks on American foreign policy in southeast Asia during the sixties and early seventies. Haldeman's Forever War and Le Guin's The Word For World Is Forest are clearly "displaced" or "sublimated" hostility directed at the same target as Darkovan "clingfire" is. This is not to say that it is psychologically "sick" to disapprove of war, only that it is psychologically healthy to express disapproval or whatever emotion seems to consume one's psychic energies.

There are, no doubt, some "neurotic" pressures that Bradley relieves by writing about certain subjects in certain ways. There is little question, for instance, that the little girl who was too short to make her way to and from elementary school in the deep snows of an upstate New York winter is subconsciously present when Bradley's narrative persona describes the cold and snowbound winters that most Darkovans experience. Such psychoanalytic insights are, however, reductionist: a true Freudian would have us believe that her childhood experience with snow is the only reason for Bradley's depiction of Darkovan blizzards. Since James Fenimore Cooper incorporates equally vivid winter scenes in The Pioneers, are we to believe that he too had some unpleasant childhood experiences in upstate New York? Or that the general vicinity (near Albany and Cooperstown) gives rise to some sort of snow-phobia? This psychoanalytic approach may interest a few, but to look for people's neuroses in the literature they write is to play a parlor game that is self-defeating. One can never be sure that such amateur psychoanalysis is right, and such an approach can easily lead away from the enjoyment of literature itself. (12) So, while some part of her writing serves private psychological needs, one may assume safely that the impetus to write--the imperative often described as a compulsion or obsession--comes from deep within the psyche and is nothing more than an indicator of what sort of psyche Marion Zimmer Bradley has. Even here, analysis breaks down: is she a "verbal" person? Then, what does "verbal" mean, for she is also quite well acquainted with the "mathematical" or "scientific" aspects of things. Since no one has successfully been able to define artistic genius, much less throw in the last words on "obsessions" and "compulsions," it is silly to try here. It is sufficient to realize that a writer writes because he or she needs to; if further inquiry is in order, it might best start with why the individual reader needs to read. These two "needs" are analogues.

Yet there is a second reason for Bradley's writing, one that takes "need" and applies it to the economic facts of life. It is all very well to "need to achieve" but it is difficult if not impossible to live without some source of income. Bradley is no stranger to the kind of writing that puts food on the table and pays the rent.

During her teens, Bradley wrote because she was psychologically so disposed. Creating fantasy worlds is fun, but it is far more satisfying to translate the imagined world into words; by pinning it down in written form, the fantasist (very loose use of the term here) makes possible the sharing of her world with others. Moreover, the fantasy in written form is liable to criticism: inconsistencies show up, improbabilities become evident, characters may seem too good, too evil, or not full enough. Once the imagined world is put on paper, the writer may return to it critically to expunge its flaws and to improve anything that needs improvement. Once this process has begun, the person who fantasizes other worlds begins to be a "writer." Before she had finished high school, Marion Zimmer the writer had evolved from the teenager who liked to imagine other worlds and "what if"s.

Most writers are directly or indirectly subsidized. Either they work at something relatively mindless and use work-time to incubate the stories they will write down when they are home, or they have wage-earning spouses whose jobs not only buy the groceries but also buy the writers enough free time to write. For most of the duration of her first marriage, Marion Zimmer Bradley belonged to the latter group; when she separated from her husband and moved to Abilene to continue her college education, she began to write pseudonymous "romance novels" to pay her own way. When she remarried and had two children, there was an interval during which her second husband was ill; at that time she would review a book for $15 and then sell the review copy to help pay the rent. (13) Marion Zimmer Bradley is no stranger to the literal meaning of "write for a living."

What is fascinating at present is that her Darkover novels—at one time the "serious writing," the time for which she had to purchase by producing two-hundred-page "romances," each with five nicely spaced romantic scenes—are at one and the same time commercial enterprises and profound expressions of deeply-held personal values. Before continuing an introduction to Marion Zimmer Bradley, the science-fiction writer, a fairly close and essentially appreciative look at her most famous writing is in order.

NOTES

1. The official date of publication for Web of Light is February 1983, but the book was available in January. Though the official date of publication for The Mists of Avalon is 18 January 1983—officially before the other—the Knopf book was unavailable, unless one had placed an order for it before publication, until it was reprinted. Such sales here prompted an unprecedented first-edition printing of 32,000 copies in England. These figures exclude Book Club editions.
2. Faren Miller, Locus, January 1983, p. 8.
3. I use the term persona to identify those aspects

of personality that Bradley--or any author--imaginatively combines and then projects to be the apparent source of her literary productions. I explain the term and the concept it represents later in this chapter. Here, I want primarily to emphasize that, where my chief concern is biography, I refer to the real person Marion Zimmer Bradley was and is; where I concern myself with the apparent source of her fiction--as I do throughout most of this book--"MZB" is my designation of the authorial persona, the literary alter ego.

4. The human male's "more acute sex drive" in this context refers only to physiological phenomena; men are fully aroused more quickly and more often than women, but women, once fully aroused, remain that way for a considerably longer time. With regard to anxiety-related sexual needs, most men and women behave the way that millions of years of mammalian evolution dictate: to survive (or to pass his genes on to the next generation), the male must persist in his efforts to mate; the female's mating behavior is nearly the opposite, since she must refuse all potential mates but the one she deems most suitable. In situations of anxiety, therefore, the human male is likely to fall back on the genetically-reinforced pattern of persistence, and the human female on that of refusal.

5. Ursula K. Le Guin, The Left Hand of Darkness. (New York: Ace Books), in 1976 and later reprintings.

6. This statement about Jaelle and Peter is a paraphrase; it and the following inference about Bradley's technocratic leanings come from a March 1979 conversation with the author in her home.

7. Private correspondence, June 1983.

8. The dedication appears on the page immediately preceding the "Prologue" (New York: Ace Books, 1971).

9. The following anecdote comes from a conversation in Bradley's home in March 1979.

10. Private correspondence, June 1983.

11. The reference is to McCaffrey's novel, To Ride Pegasus (New York: Ballantine Books, 1973); the novel is about the use of psychic powers, so the mythical winged horse suggests the imagination in flight yet in control.

12. The two greatest American poets, Dickinson and Whitman, have had their works psychoanalyzed to such a degree that criticism of their poetry illuminates "reclu-

38

siveness" and "homosexuality" far more often than it helps readers to appreciate the greatness of their poems. More often than not, such "criticism" is more revealing of the critics than of the poets or poems being criticized.

13. Private correspondence, August 1979.

III

SURVEYING DARKOVER

Out there somewhere, situated ideally between our solar system and the other planets populated by our fictional descendants, there is a red dwarf star. Its habitable planet is known to the Terrans who use its main spaceport as a transfer and refueling stop merely as Cottman IV. To the thousands of science-fiction readers who have experienced life under that blood-red sun by having read all or any of eighteen related novels and ten formally published stories by Marion Zimmer Bradley, that world is Darkover. In a whimsical mood, Bradley speaks of her planet as a kind of imaginary playground, a place to read about for fun when one is in the mood for innocuous fantasy. When she is serious, however, Bradley admits that Darkover has come to have so real an existence that she can "tamper with it only at (her) own peril." (1) This chapter is analogous to both a travel agent's brochure and the report by a survey team who describe not geophysical but psychological phenomena. Its end is not literary criticism in the usual sense; rather, it is a pre-critical exploration of what the Darkover writings are and are about. This chapter aims at guiding the reader toward an appreciation of Marion Zimmer Bradley's central imaginative activity, the sustained creation of a world, its peoples, and their complex interactions.

Bradley initially created Darkover when she was a teenager; after The Planet Savers and The Sword of Aldones ("al DOE nays") were published as an Ace double in 1962, her readers and the judgment of Donald A. Wollheim practically forced her to write more science fiction set on the planet. Initially, Bradley felt that she was taking advantage of some good luck--that she was not really exercising her creativity enough--by writing again and again about characters and incidents on the same fictional world. Gradually, though, she came to realize not only that there was a ready market for books about Darkover but also that her frequent returns to the same setting constituted a serious "thought-experiment." That is, by setting the action on a world that already had a fictional existence, she found that she could test various ideas (blithely accepted or unthinkingly condemned) of here-and-now Earthly origin by letting them be put into action by characters not bound by our own values and social conditioning.

"Is Gender Necessary?" was written by Ursula Le Guin to explain the rationale behind her creation of an ambisexual human race in The Left Hand of Darkness. She describes the literary existence of her Gethenians as an experiment:

Because of our lifelong social conditioning, it is hard for us to see clearly what, besides purely physiological form and function, truly differentiates men and women. Are there real differences in temperament, capacity, talent, psychic processes, etc.? If so, what are they?....How to find out?...One can send an imaginary...man into an imaginary culture which is totally free of sex roles....I eliminated gender, to find out what was left. Whatever was left would be, presumably, simply human. (2)

We need change this passage only slightly to describe Darkover. Delete sexual physiology and sex roles, insert "now-latent psychic powers"; replace "elimated gender" with "enhanced psionic ability," change "what was left" to "what was gained"; and substitute for "simply" a phrase like "more fully" (human). Darkover is not only one occurrence of the thought-experimentation that Le Guin says science fiction is all about: it is the experiment multiplied, replicated and constantly monitored, and possibly of unequalled magnitude.

It began when Marion Zimmer wrote about "the Seveners," in the unpublished King and the Sword at the age of fifteen. Interested in psychology as it really applies to humans, she postulated a world whose dominant families or dynasties were each gifted with a particular psionic talent: thus seven families, seven distinct psi-talents. How would the groups of people, the individual persons, and the particular psionic abilities interrelate? Although it was never published, this novel influenced The Sword of Aldones and contained some exploration of human psionic potentialities; these were altered and refined in the young woman's subconscious musings, and early speculations about special psychological abilities continued to grow toward maturity.

In 1958 "The Planet Savers" appeared as a novelette in Amazing; in it, MZB incorporates two psychological oddities. The main character, Dr. Jason Allison, is a textbook example of a "split personality," and Regis Hastur ("RAY jes HAH stir") exemplifies a true Darkovan telepath. From this printed beginning in Amazing, on through the Ace double four years later, to Darkover Landfall--which Donald Wollheim retitled so that "Darkover" would draw sales from what he knew to be a large number of readers wanting another Dark-over novel--Marion Zimmer Bradley's thought-experiment stea-dily gathered momentum. And, as Darkover grew in complexi-ty, it drew more and more readers--many because of the implications embedded in the fiction, others because of the quality of the story-telling itself.

The following lists Bradley's fictions according to the sequence of incidents as they happen on Darkover:

Darkover Landfall
Stormqueen!
Hawkmistress!
Two to Conquer
"The Sword of Chaos"
"The Legend of Lady Bruna"
"To Keep the Oath"
"The Waterfall"
The Shattered Chain (part 1)
"The Keeper's Price"
"The Lesson of the Inn"
The Spell Sword
The Forbidden Tower
(The Shattered Chain, parts 2 & 3)
Thendara House
"Thendara House"
City of Sorcery
Star of Danger
"Oathbreaker"
"The Hawk-Master's Son"

The Winds of Darkover
The Bloody Sun
The Heritage of Hastur
The Planet Savers
Sharra's Exile
"Blood Will Tell"
The Sword of Aldones
The World Wreckers

This sequential listing is not absolutely precise, since MZB wrote the works as independent, separate fictions. The temporal setting of The Shattered Chain, for example, contains a "pause" of twelve years during which all the incidents of The Spell Sword--a novel published two years previously--occur. It is certain, from what The Spell Sword reveals about Callista, that "The Lesson of the Inn" is set several years before that novel begins; the same story, likewise, suggests that "The Keeper's Price" (as its incidents occur on Darkover) precedes it.

But "To Keep the Oath," because it is only tenuously related to "The Waterfall," can be read as if it were set at the same time without damaging the sense of Darkover. Both stories are set well before the first part of The Shattered Chain. Since Rohana Ardais is only a girl in "The Waterfall" and Kindra n'ha Mhari already a mature woman in "To Keep the Oath," it is likely that "To Keep the Oath" takes place first. Further, the opening scenes of The Shattered Chain show Camilla "nearing middle age"; she was about twenty in "To Keep the Oath," and Kindra was fifteen to twenty years her senior. Yet Kindra seems only slightly older than Rohana in The Shattered Chain. But the story and the novel are separate fictions, and it is unlikely that Kindra in her mid-fifties (her necessary age at the beginning of The Shattered Chain if one follows the chronology of "To Keep the Oath") would still be working as a mercenary soldier. With further investigation, the complexities only grow: far better to enjoy the fictions as autonomous!

"Blood Will Tell" revised only slightly begins the second chapter of Sharra's Exile and as story and chapter precedes The Sword of Aldones. Yet these two novels are, for all readers but the most meticulous, set at the same time. Thus the list here is only a guide; readers for whom the exact sequence is important are very likely those who will reread and reread and then adjust the setting of a story or part of a novel by a year or two to suit themselves.

Once the popularity of the DAW-published Darkover novels made Bradley's name commercially valuable, Ace Books began reissuing some of her early out-of-print titles. Among these were The Door Through Space and Falcons of Narabedla, neither of which is a Darkover novel. Because they were reprinted along with some early works about Darkover and because an important science-fiction reference guide lists them as Darkover novels, they require a brief explanation. (3)

Falcons of Narabedla was published originally in five successive issues of Harlan Ellison's fanzine Dimensions, beginning in 1954. Ten years later it became one half of an Ace double (the other half was a collection of MZB's short stories). According to Bradley, it is not worth reading, although one can see in its use of psionics a suggestion of the teleportation of human beings important to the plots of Sharra's Exile, The Sword of Aldones, and Two to Conquer. Bradley is probably correct; the main feature of the novel is the psi-kidnapping, by mutant telepaths of the far future, of an Earthman whose former life is fictionally almost contemporary with ours. Unless one is told that the novel is set entirely on Earth or unless one reads very carefully, it is easy to assume (with hindsight) that the kidnappers are Darkovans.

Neither does The Door Through Space, according to Bradley, deserve to be read; her assessment: "Perhaps not quite as bad as Falcons." (4) First published as a novel in 1961, The Door Through Space is unquestionably set on the planet Wolf, not Darkover. At the time, evidently, Bradley thought she had finished publishing about Darkover with the novelette, "Planet Savers." Thus, she took a "leftover" part of the Darkover in her mind and perhaps in her earlier, unpublished writings--the settings of the Dry Towns--and made use of it in the world of The Door Through Space. Later, of course, Bradley realized that Darkover could not so easily be disposed of: the Dry Towns belong on Darkover and nowhere else. That they were pressed into service in this early novel is unfortunate--for The Door Through Space.

If, however, readers follow Bradley's advice--to look upon these early works as juvenilia too imitative of the work of C. L. Moore and Henry Kuttner and therefore best forgotten--they can "forget" the novels themselves yet at the same time "remember" that powerful psionic abilities and settings like the Dry Towns on Wolf were never very far from the working consciousness of MZB. These two undistinguished novels may be regarded as manifestations of the abiding presence of Darkover in Bradley's unconscious yet active imagination.

Since the present discussion is part of a "Reader's Guide," suggestions about the order in which to read the Darkover novels are not entirely tangential. The list several pages back indicates the internal sequence of the Darkover fictions (see Appendix A for their history of publication). Internal chronology, however, is not an order to be obeyed blindly; the best advice is not to follow that sequence. One reason for not reading Darkover Landfall first is that it takes the mystery away from a good part of the other books. That is, Darkover Landfall may not give it all away, but it certainly explains much that thoughtful readers should be wondering about as they read some of the other books first. Another valid reason is that Darkover Landfall is a better book than some of those published earlier. If one reads it before early novels like The Planet Savers and The Sword of Aldones, these novels written earlier are bound to be disappointing--in the how-well-they-are-written sense--when compared with a novel written ten years later. Finally, Marion Zimmer Bradley prefers that the Darkover books be read in the order in which they were written; that way, the reader can follow the actual development not only of Bradley's writing skills but also of the complexities that grow as Darkover is explored in ever-increasing depth and subtlety.

If readers are moderately experienced, they can enjoy reading almost any kind of science fiction by noting the copyright date of a story or novel and then making allowances for its lack of sophistication according to present standards. Thus, it is "natural" that the first edition of The Bloody Sun is not nearly so good--as literature or as skill with language--as the more recently published longer novels. Some readers, however, ought not to follow this particular approach, but neither should everyone do as Bradley suggests and read the Darkover novels in the order of their publication. If one reads The Sword of Aldones first, for instance, one will miss a number of good things simply because of a lack of familiarity with Darkover; during a second reading, or if one has read other Darkover novels earlier, these good things stand out.

If one adopts a "remember when it was written" frame of mind to compare it with the two other novels--Dick's Man in the High Castle and Piper's Little Fuzzy--that were running neck-and-neck for the Hugo Award that year, one can see weaknesses in its conclusion not very noticeable at a first reading. Still, it is tempting to second-guess that final ballot: Bradley's unselfish politicking for Little Fuzzy may well have lost her a Hugo, even though a second reading discloses some real problems in the consclusion of Sword of Aldones. Whatever the novel's "absolute" merits, it is going to puzzle the new-to-Darkover reader--just as it will not confuse someone who has read, for instance, The Heritage of Hastur and The Winds of Darkover.

So, striking a compromise between Bradley's suggestion and that of a hypothetical "strict chronologist," here are some suggestions for those who want to begin to read the Darkover novels. If one enjoys the earlier work of Heinlein--the "space-adventure" novels--then Star of Danger may be a good beginning, followed by The Spell Sword. If one seeks more than just adventure, it may be best to postpone Star of Danger and begin with The Spell Sword, for the latter novel is on one level good sword-and-sorcery and on another a very carefully written story that takes the sorcery out of the realm of the fantastic and pins it down to plausible extrapolation from the science of psychology. After The Spell Sword, its sequel, The Forbidden Tower, or any of the "big books"--from The Heritage of Hastur on-- should be sufficient preparation for yielding to temptation and discovering, in Darkover Landfall, quite a few of the answers to questions that the other books have raised.

One qualification here, however: men who are not particularly infatuated by women's liberation ought not to read The Shattered Chain as the first of the "big books." This novel is the story of three women, centers on the rescue of a man by two of these women (reverses the damsel-in-distress

cliche), explores in detail the group of Darkovan women
called Free Amazons, and turns out to be one of the most
sensitive and realistic treatments of "liberation" and "free
choice" in science fiction. On the other hand, all women
and self-admitted "male chauvinists" (open admission is
usually a sign of self-directed humor and of a secretly open
mind) "must" include The Shattered Chain among the first of
the longer and more recent Darkover novels. (The emphasis
on this novel is hardly special pleading for a feminist
point of view; the emphasis arises, rather, from currently
widespread misinformation about the nature of feminism--
especially in the 1980's--and from the facts that its author
is not a feminist and that the novel will, whatever the
reader thinks and feels, either confirm one's position or
else be upsetting enough to enforce some serious thinking.)

Nor should the recently-published Thendara House be
read at the beginning of one's survey of Darkover. More
than any other, this Darkover novel is a sequel. It takes
up the story of Jaelle and Magda almost from the point at
which the earlier novel ends. More important, its imagery--
scenes any reader of The Shattered Chain will recognize--is
all to likely to confuse a new reader, even if he or she is
already familiar with the hallucinations that beset newly-
awakening telepaths. The novel is without question a major
one, for one of its thematic explorations is the degree to
which personal liberty and development can be subordinated
to the values of a group, but it is best left until one has
read The Shattered Chain.

Meanwhile, back in orbit around that red star....Marion
Zimmer Bradley's Darkover books are not a series; they are
simply a number of stories set on the same planet. Their
author seems in profound agreement with Emerson's truism
about consistency's being the hobgoblin of little minds.
She is not writing a future history and believes that it is
her right as an artist to have the story she is telling
dictate that a journey from here to there requires two days
of travel, even though in another book the same trip made at
the same speed takes at least twice as long.

According to Bradley, The Bloody Sun is her essential
work about Darkover. It contains the seeds of what happens
on the planet afterwards and the results of what has happened on the planet previously. When it was first published

47

in 1964, the science-fiction publishing "establishment" had inherited from the pulp magazines a "rule" about length; apparently, no science-fiction narrative exceeding two hundred pages would suit the taste of readers. So, The Bloody Sun of 1964 was not really the novel that MZB had written: initially, it was longer, and then it was cut by Ace Books to a more suitable length. As one reads that first edition, one can sense those editorial cuts--there seem to be little gaps in the story and certain characters behave in ways for which the reader has had no preparation--but, especially if reading the book for the first time, one attributes the lack of continuity and character development to a corresponding lack of skill on the part of the author.

The new Bloody Sun (1979) is an edition with all those earlier cuts restored and with additional material added to the original novel. Because of the books she had published in the interval between these two editions, MZB is able to make the narrative the center of things Darkovan. In 1979-- as she could not in 1964--MZB knows what happened to Damon Ridenow ("REED 'n oh") and his Forbidden Tower; she knows why Kennard Alton has become an embittered man; she knows in detail what effects the presence of Terran technology has had on the traditional uses of matrixes in the Towers; and she knows a lot of other details besides. MZB's revision of The Bloody Sun puts the essence of the earlier version solidly into the Darkovan scheme of things; it also brings to the basic story a maturity of prose style that the earlier edition lacked. As Donald Wollheim has said on several occasions, Bradley is "a real pro"; and the least one can expect from such a writer is a marked growth as a literary artist over an interval of fifteen years. One's expectations are not disappointed.

According to Bradley, "the direct inspiration" for The Bloody Sun is the quotation from Franz Werfel's The Star of the Unborn that appears before the prologue: "The stranger who comes home does not make himself at home but makes home strange." (5) She has written that the "germ" of the novel--in fact, of all her books--is a bit of a poem by A. E. Houseman: "I, a stranger and afraid / In a world I never made." (6) The poem is a lament of alienation. The speaker tells of discovering, in the cosmos to which he formerly thought he belonged by right of birth, that there are "laws"---of God and of Man--that do not fairly apply to his condition. Although he had no part in making them and finds them irrelevant to his own situation, he learns that he is expected to obey these laws without question. Quite understandably, the speaker feels frustrated and alienated from the world of which he once thought himself a part. The Bloody Sun tells of Jeff Kerwin's nearly frustrated attempt to find a place for himself on Darkover, the world of his birth but not, because he was brought up in the Terrans' Spacemen's Orphanage there, the world of which he is a citizen.

Most of MZB's books published before 1980 (but including Sharra's Exile, and City of Sorcery too) spring from that same "germ." The usual plot is concerned with the relationship between a tradition-bound Darkovan society and a techno-maniacal Terran Empire. Given the complexity with which MZB has treated both cultures, there is conflict enough in that relationship for several novels. To make real this conflict and to add a distinctly personal and emotional quality to her works, MZB usually focuses on a "lost" or "strange" Terran and his Darkovan acquaintances who later become more than his friends. The man or boy from the Terran Empire is some kind of misfit; he is usually in need of something emotional that the Terran community cannot provide.

He finds it--whatever it is: friendship, understanding, lasting love, a sense of home--among characters who are usually more liberal and less xenophobic than the average Darkovan. By the end of each novel, the misfit finds his place, but he has to pay dearly for what he seeks and gets, for Darkover is a planet with a culture that accepts outsiders only on its own terms. The price is steep, but the reward is Darkover; and Darkover has and is whatever it takes to cause a considerable number of science-fiction readers to regard it as a second home.

Despite Bradley's refusal to have Darkover pinned down by maps and despite her frequently exasperating (and exasperated) "Oh, it's fantasy, not science fiction" response to questions about minor inconsistencies, Darkover is the result of some very careful thought about astronomy and physics as well as about the inner motivations of psychologically realistic characters. Most of the Darkover novels

take place about three thousand Earth years in the future;
(7) the Terran Empire--with its emphasis on technology,
commerce, and progress--is a reasonable extrapolation from
Western culture.

Similarly, the geophysical aspects of Darkover, except
its variously-colored moons, are well within the range of
plausibility. The moons, Bradley says, result from her only
"completely non-scientific idea" about the plausibility of
her created world. (8) Yet, as Henry James is said to have
noted about "accidents" in fiction--that they will ruin the
work of a novice, but somehow will enhance a true artist's
work--those arbitrarily-colored moons of Darkover can almost
withstand scientific scrutiny because even now one cannot
dismiss out of hand the possibility that our own moon was
"captured" by the Earth's gravity. Had Bradley chosen other
colors (the blue-green part of the spectrum cannot be light
originating in a red sun), the moons of Darkover just could
have been asteroids that passed to close to the planet, and
the planetary system is certainly old enough for them to
have established stable orbits.

One of the most obvious features of the Darkovan land-
scape is the "bloody sun." If MZB's red sun were a red
giant, her planet would be a cinder inside the star, so
Darkover's primary is a red dwarf. Because it is, Darkover
can be an incredibly ancient world on which there has been
plenty of time for geophysical change, evolutionary development, and climatic alteration. "Plenty of time" encompasses
billions of years--if our own solar system is fairly repre-
sentative--and, during those eons, as much as was learned
could easily have been forgotten: Homo sapiens is practically ephemeral in the history of our own planet, so one cannot
realistically expect even the ancient Chieri ("chee AIR ee")
to know everything about their aging world. Concerning
Darkover, there are many gaps in knowledge, gaps that MZB
puts to her own artistic uses.

One phenomenon allowed by the extreme age of Darkover
is the possibility of several species' evolution to a human-
like level of sentience. We know that elephants and toothed
whales have brains very similar to ours; who knows what will
become of them if we not destroy their habitats or hunt them
to extinction? Quite reasonably, then, Darkover could have
been home to a number of different sapient native species

50

before the first humans arrived.

Since water is as important as heat and light to carbon-based life forms, these several species can believably have migrated, over millions of years, to regions of high elevation where enormously tall mountains draw precipitation down onto their slopes and nearby foothills and high country. The height and shape of the Hellers, as the mountains are called, suggest that they are geologically young (our Rockies and Sierras are only about thirty million years old). This relative youth, in turn, makes it feasible that radically different intelligent life forces--the Ya-men, Catfolk, Trailmen, and Chieri--could have arisen in various eras and in different locations and have lived near the Hellers during too brief a geological time for one of them to have established itself as the single dominant species on the planet.

Another peculiarity about Darkover is the resistance of the habitable regions to accurate cartography, a peculiarity that is convenient to MZB's preference for the autonomy of each of the stories in the "series" and also one that has a solid geophysical foundation. When the people of the Terran Empire arrive, they are unable to use aircraft safely in the vicinity of the Hellers because of convection currents, rapidly shifting winds, the almost perpetual blizzards in winter, the cloud cover that accompanies them, and the sudden rainstorms in summer. Yet Darkovan civilization is concentrated by biological necessity near these mountains, so aerial and satellite mapping of the entire planet is possible but of very little practicality. Thus the geography of the inhabited parts of the planet, while consistent with both geology and climatology, nevertheless remains uncertain enough for MZB to leave credible gaps in everyone's knowledge, so that her "inconsistencies" become irrelevant.

Darkover's sun, from a Terran point of view an insignificant star, is also carefully located by MZB: it is a star with a planetary system (so that some permanent spaceport is possible), a star located at a point in the galactic spiral that is a convenient stopover for spacecraft traveling from one arm of the galaxy to another. The Terrans care little about the planet and its inhabitants themselves; what the Terrans see and want is control of a planet ideally located for transfers of cargo and passengers and for repairs of their great interstellar fleet.

What the Terrans cannot understand is the reluctance of the Darkovans to have their homeworld so used. Neither can they understand the nearly phobic reaction by most Darkovans to the Terrans' machines and and even weapons as simple as a handgun. The Darkovans live what appears superficially to be a very simple, almost feudal kind of life. Although some have extraordinary mental talents, they settle disagreements by means of the old-fashioned duel. To the Terrans, the Darkovans are "undeveloped" and ridiculously fixated on the benighted notion that Terran "progress" is a path that will lead to cultural suicide.

What the Terrans do not realize is that Darkovan civilization is dying of old age. The inherited psionic talents of the six major families (whose territories are called Domains) are no longer so prevalent, and the families themselves are genetically fragile as a result of previous inbreeding. The seventh Domain has been banished from the Comyn (the group of Darkovans still in possession of telepathic abilities) for some grave crime committed perhaps millennia in the past. While the Terrans regard this family--the Aldarans--as among the most progressive and open-minded, the Terrans do not know that the Aldarans' crime was related to bellicose use of psi powers as well as of long-range weapons.

In its youth, long before the Terran Empire came to be, Darkovan society nearly annihilated itself during the Ages of Chaos with a centuries-long equivalent of a biochemical and nuclear war. The survivors agreed to the terms of the Darkovan Compact: that no one would ever again use psychic power against another for harm and that no one would attack another in a physical way that left the attacker safe from the defenses of his intended victim. Hand-to-hand combat, swordfighting, and similar kinds of aggression were tolerated, for they give the attacked a fair chance of repelling or destroying the attacker. When the first of the Terran Empire ships arrived on Darkover, its crew regarding gun-like hand weapons as quite ordinary, it was only natural that most Darkovans saw the Terrans as utterly dangerous. If these strangers considered guns to be ordinary, they obviously considered the value of human life an expendable cost. Remembering their own Ages of Chaos, engendered by Terran-like thinking with regard to weapons and the taking of life, the Darkovans looked upon the Terrans' offer of "progress" as a promise to help them succeed at the self-destruction they had escaped just barely. The traditional Darkovan was quite satisfied to adhere to the Compact, especially when conscious of its alternative.

One major element of the Darkover novels with temporal settings after that of The Shattered Chain is the conflict between two ways of life. One is more advanced but essentially similar to our own technocracy; the other is apparently primitive but basically in harmony with the ecology of the aging world. This conflict is thematically a source of social analysis (of our present ways) and critical commentary, but MZB refuses to allow her works to wander into politics unless true concerns of realistic characters bring them there. Her emphasis is on character, not political themes.

MZB's treatment of the character of Regis Hastur exemplifies her subordination of theme to character. Regis appears in a number of the Darkover novels, and even so early as The Planet Savers and The Sword of Aldones, he is an accomplished (though still developing) political leader. There is something about him--and this is the result of MZB's mastery of characterization--that intrigues the reader; for instance, Regis is not really likable in The Heritage of Hastur unless one has met him in The Planet Savers or The Sword of Aldones previously, or until one encounters him during a second reading of Heritage. Still, one may follow his political aspirations and even be interested in them, but first and always one is interested in Regis Hastur the "person."

All of MZB's themes are similarly embodied in the actions and motivations of her characters. Part of her being "a real pro" is her ability to create believable characters and to tell a good story about them. Bard di Asturien of Two to Conquer is exemplary. His motives and attitudes are almost thoroughly detestable, and we cannot really like him no matter how many times we read the book. Yet MZB's treatment of his character keeps him always this side of being a type-cast villain: unpleasant in the extreme, he still holds our interest. So, despite what some readers see as too much "message"--of course there are important themes in the books--MZB's narratives are first, second, third, and fourth just good stories about interesting characters; theme would find a place on that list somewhere near ninth or tenth.

All the foregoing does not, however, explain what Darkover is: what about it causes readers and author to return to what is basically an inhospitable world? For Darkover is not a place to visit, even vicariously, the way one vacations in some sunny tourist spot. Darkover is cold. And, in the Dry Towns away from the mountains, Darkover is hot, dusty, and dry. The great mountains, the Hellers (named because of the hellish difficulty they pose for any traveler), are central to Darkover, for in their heights they gather moisture to be sent through dense forests toward the arable high country in snow-fed rivers and streams. Except in high summer, nightly rains turn to sleet and snow. The climate and topography overcome even the fierce self-sufficiency of the Darkovans to the extent that "shelter truce" is sacred.

This truce is, by the time of The Shattered Chain--the novel which is the earliest of those set in the "modern era" (9)--so necessary and natural a part of Darkovan culture that its origins are forgotten. Like most laws of survival, it is simple: travelers forced to share a shelter during bad weather--no matter what their individual or political inclinations--may not harm other persons similarly stranded. Along the roads and trails in the high country, there are crude but sturdy shelters for people and their animals, and these are usually stocked with some provisions and blankets against the possibility of a traveler's being caught in a fierce snowstorm. Inside the shelter, there must be no violence. Should a person break the shelter truce, he or she is publicly declared an outlaw; considering the difficulty of staying alive on Darkover under normal circumstances, being outlawed by the equivalent of an entire nation is tantamount to being sentenced to certain death.

Other integral aspects of Darkover are, for natives of the planet, the knowledge that one's actions really count, an inalienable sense of home, and, quite frequently, the ability to communicate telepathically. In what passes for society on Earth today, there is a widespread feeling of

54

powerlessness: those of us fortunate not to be starving in third-world countries are far too often just social security numbers with credit ratings, or something similarly impersonal, to all but our good friends. Darkovan life offers a contrast to our present situation. Darkovans are fiercely autonomous; what differentiates them is not a number nor even a retinal pattern but something more personal. On Darkover, a world that was never suited to human habitation, those who would like to be able to do something find a place where day-to-day survival is nearly heroic activity.

Related to this yearning for effective action is what the sociologists and psychologists tell us: that our own culture is made up of great numbers of alienated individuals. The "nuclear family"--partly the result of midcentury affluence and partly the effect on "extended familes" of national and multi-national corporations' transfers of personnel across the country and across the world--has proved an emotional and psychological failure. Instead of the closeness of mother, father, and their children held up as an ideal by misinformed "traditionalists," the woman who works in the home is practically isolated there, the man who works outside the home is kept by the demands of his occupation from spending enough time with his wife and children, and the children must adapt to short-term acquaintanceships instead of friendships because their father's job has made relocation a way of life. Now that two-thirds of married women work outside the home as well, this "family" has been in practice redefined as the adults and their children who sleep (most of the time, anyway) in the same house or apartment. "Home" seems an abstraction.

On Darkover, by contrast, there are all manner of formal and informal long-term relationships. In the Domains, at least, the average child spends her or his childhood with biological parents and then, more often than not, is "fostered" with some relative until he or she reaches adulthood. Kinship--whether biological or bloodsworn--is important, at every stage of life. And, since kinship is defined ultimately by the settlement-place of post-Landfall families, all Darkovans have at least one geographic location to which they are psychologically and emotionally bound. There is, of course, the matter of arranged marriage and the prospect that a father will not acknowledge his sometimes numerous illegitimate children. There is for women sometimes only the hope that they will bear male children before the rigors of childbirth end their lives; there is for men a similarly desperate hope that their family positions and physical attributes combine to let them live their lives according to their preferences. Although these aspects of family life on Darkover are hardly pleasant, their existence in an alternate universe makes them the more attractive. As long as one is _reading_ about Darkover, not experiencing it, one's "what if"s regarding home and family are likely to be positive, both larger and warmer than in "real life."

Besides the rootlessness for which Darkover offers an alternative and despite the implications of our planet-wide news media, we seem to need a remedy for "lack of communication." On Darkover we find the Comyn ("KOE min"), people who are trained to make use of their mental energies and who, under the proper circumstances, can communicate telepathically far more accurately than anyone can with impotent words. Estrangements caused by our all-too-frequent "But I don't understand" are rare events indeed on Darkover.

The other side of telepathic talent—the estrangement caused by a person's understanding all too well what another is meaning—is also a fact of Darkovan life. MZB's portrayal of telepathic communication may be a deduction arrived at upon consideration of what mind-to-mind contact must involve, or it may be an extrapolation of the sensitivity we know to exist among dolphins and porpoises. These intelligent marine mammals not only use sounds to communicate volitionally but also possess so fine an auditory-tactile sensitivity that they can "hear" the heartbeats and digestive processes of those around them; they need never ask so silly a question as "How are you?" Whatever the evidence drawn upon to create her Darkovan telepaths, MZB quite reasonably endows them with considerably less privacy than we humans have; this psychic transparency, in turn, permits her to reveal characters' motives and attitudes—and their reactions to what others are thinking—without straining the reader's credulity at all.

The relationships among Darkovan telepaths and the internal conflicts each must undergo before reaching maturity are themselves interesting; they are also metaphorical examinations of the growth toward self-knowledge experienced by every sensitive human being. Darkovans' attempts to come to terms with who they are (for who they are is evident to other telepaths even if it is not to a self-deluding or immature Darkovan) provide an extremely rich vein of material for story-telling and a most powerful symbol of the process of self-integration. On Darkover, the awakening of psionic talent occurs usually at puberty; for us, adolescence is that interval in our lives during which each of us attempts first to define her or himself by rebelling against whatever "they" say is the "correct behavior" and second by experimenting with the various "selves" we are, seeking to find the one or the combination of ones that will let us be the persons we want to become.

For Darkovans, this awakening of psi energy--especially as it occurs at the same time the young Darkovan is becoming sexually mature--is a tremendous psychical and emotional upheaval. Laran, as the psi-powers are called, is the kind of gift the payment for which is often years of disciplined training. Since many young readers of science fiction are, from the point of view of their conventionally socialized peers, "out of it"--are more intelligent, more introspective, more vulnerable to emotional assaults and therefore more liable to withdraw into the safer world of read-about experience--they find in the difficulties of young Darkovan telepaths not just imaginary company but the promise that their own emotional experiences will, when they have passed out of adolescence and into adulthood, have prepared them for a life psychologically and emotionally more satisfying than the day-to-day existence of the contemporary Everyman, whom Bradley sometimes categorizes as "Joe Six-pack."

The paranormal psychic abilities with which MZB endows her Darkovans are imaginary phenomena that suggest real analogues with ethical consequences, but they are also interesting in themselves. One of the members of the Comyn, the Alton family, has the power of forced rapport. An Alton can read her or his way into another's mind whether or not the other consents, and the rage of an Alton who has lost her or his temper and with it control of psychic output can literally kill the person at whom it is directed.

Before and during the Ages of Chaos, the Hasturs evidently bred into themselves a laran that enabled a Hastur mind to transcend temporal barriers, to "see" not only into the past but into the future as well. It seems, however, that the stronger the "gift," the less likely would it be for the Hastur "seer" to differentiate between past and present, future and past, and present and future. Moreover, when the _laran_ was really powerful, the Hastur mind was unable to distinguish among "futures" of greatly varying probabilities. Thus Allart Hastur, one of the chief characters in _Stormqueen!_, goes nearly insane because of the myriad possibilities--each equally real to him--that push aside his normal consciousness at erratic and frequent intervals.

On Darkover, it is obviously necessary to learn to control one's _laran_. Normally such education and training take place in a Tower where there are expert telepaths to teach not only control but maximum use of whatever a young Darkovan's psychic gift happens to be. If the young person has _laran_ to an extraordinary degree, it is likely that he or she will spend a lifetime in one of the Towers, for only those with especially strong psi-powers, together with necessarily strong mental and physical discipline, can safely use the matrixes that are at once the very reason for the Towers' existence and the source of Darkover's unique "technology."

The long years during which the materials and subjects of Bradley's Darkovan thought-experiment were incubating--and the value of so thorough a sub-, semi-, and fully-conscious preparation--are evident in the fundamentally consistent and very detailed treatment they achieve in the Darkover novels and stories. The discussion of The Bloody Sun, some pages back, alludes to the "matrix technology" that made possible a complex civilization. The reason that the Darkovans can remain civilized on a world not only senescent but lacking any sizable concentrations of metals is the compatibility of their psi-technology with the planet's fragile ecology. During the modern era, Comyn Castle--each huge stone block of it emplaced by the coordinated effort of many gifted minds--stands opposite the Terran spaceport, a machine-made construct which, during the lifetime of Rohana Ardais, began as a bulldozed wound in the old but living earth.

It is not necessary, alas, to acquaint any readers with

what future--or contemporary--machinery can do, but it is important that the reader of Bradley's Darkover fictions understand at least the fundamentals of the matrix technology. This technological use of the human mind is cause and result of Darkovan civilization, and it is significant in a literary sense because it seems so natural to Darkover--a tribute to the complex and subtle way that Bradley gradually reveals the detailed wholeness of her created world.

Soon after there were human beings on Darkover, the use of matrixes (each a blue-tinted crystal which may be said to amplify psychic energy) began. The matrix, by nature, is unique in the universe; small ones, perhaps the size of a thumbnail, can be attuned with the psychic patterns of one, and only one, human being. The person, someone who has paranormal psychic ability or potential, first holds, then looks into, the "starstone" until he or she feels that the crystal is "vibrating" in perfect accord with her or his heartbeat, respiration, and other physical rhythms. Once this resonance is achieved, the person and stone are virtually inseparable and, indeed, "parts" of the same psychic entity.

A longstanding Darkovan tradition--dating, perhaps, from the time at which it became obvious that there were several kinds of laran and that the matrixes interacted with them--is the testing of children for potential laran. Leroni, those who have both the skill requisite for controlled use of their great psionic abilities and the willingness to dedicate their lives to service by laran, would at first (before the Ages of Chaos) tour the countryside and test every child they could. Later, when the people of the Domains had genetically established the various strains of laran, they would send their children to a Tower for testing and education in the uses of their gifts. Two reasons exist for the testing and education programs: one is that paranormal psionic abilities need to be understood sufficiently so that the psionically talented person is not at the mercy of her or his laran, and the other is that Darkovan society needs the most gifted of its members to staff the Towers which are, almost literally, the "power plants" for matrix technology.

The Towers are towers in the physical sense; their history predates the Ages of Chaos but, if the tower-like

part of the castle of Rafael di Asturien in _Two to Conquer_
is representative, the true Towers may have evolved from
such parts of a noble family's castle. That is: in _Two to
Conquer_ the reader discovers that a remote corner of the
Asturien castle is reserved, very probably because it is
remote and therefore spatially insulated from outside dis-
tractions, for the uses of _laran_ that require several well-
trained adepts to combine their psychic force. Whatever
their origin, the Towers on Darkover are places the purpose
of which is to harness the amplified _laran_ of a group of
highly skilled psionic workers.

The combination of such power is effected by matrix
screens, a construct of several large and therefore very
powerful matrixes that can be operated only by a group of
persons working together as a "circle" under the unifying
direction of a Keeper. No single person, no matter how
psionically gifted, can control the awesome powers generated
by a matrix screen. (In _The Spell Sword_ the leader of the
Catfolk tries to use a level four matrix screen--one that
properly requires a circle of at least four persons--as a
weapon and is literally burnt to a crisp by the energies he
cannot control.) In fact, because matrix work uses the same
source of energy drawn upon by sexual intimacy, members of a
circle abstain from sex during the times when they are
likely to be using the screens. Between the Ages of Chaos
and the modern era, moreover, it became traditional that
Keepers not only be celibate when they may be called on to
use their powers in a circle but that they be virgin women.
Thus, the neural channels otherwise used alternately for
matrix work and lovemaking are never in the Keeper's life
"blocked" by the flow of sexual energy.

The work of the Darkovan Towers is crucial to Darkovan
civilization. Circles working in two distant towers can
communicate instantaneously, so that in the Domains, at
least (where matrix work continues to be important, even so
late as the time during which _The World Wreckers_ is set),
neither distance nor bad weather is an impediment to communication. The Towers also function as uniquely efficient
technical centers. The psychic power generated by a high
level matrix screen, a skilled Keeper, and a circle of
powerful _leroni_ is sufficient to probe the planet's crust
for necessary ores, find them, purify them molecule by

molecule, and finally bring the required metal to the surface. Power that can perform a task of such delicacy and magnitude is power almost without limit; in several of the Darkover novels, teleportation of living persons is accomplished by use of the matrix screens.

However powerful the Darkovan matrix technology, it requires talented Keepers, monitors, and more than a few dedicated _leroni_ to keep it functional. With the arrival of the humans from the Terran Empire and their great machines, fewer and fewer Darkovans were willing to give significant portions of their lives to the discipline of the Towers.

The tradition that a Keeper could not function unless she were a virgin helped not at all. Moreover, during the modern era on Darkover, the effects of the ages-past breeding programs--those that established the various kinds of _laran_ as distinct genetic endowments--were becoming obvious. The members of Comyn families who retained their full gift were few, and fewer still were fertile, for past inbreeding was taking its toll.

The presence of sexually egalitarian Terrans on Darkover effectively undercut the sense of superiority that was the birthright of every Darkovan male. With their own psychic powers waning, with the wealth and ease and prosperity that seemed a glamour cast upon all things Terran, even their tradition that Keepers must be women seems an influence on the Darkovans' deteriorating cultural identity. Thus, the appeal of Darkover is paradoxical. Bradley seems to be aware of one side of this paradox, for she effectively put an end to Darkover with _The World Wreckers_, a novel she says she wrote "to kill off Darkover" and one in which the political supremacy of the Comyn gives way to an expectation of a new order that is not distinctly Darkovan at all. On the other hand, most of her recent Darkover novels are grounded in the older, more traditionally Darkovan way of life.

Stormqueen! (1978) tells of Darkovan life at the beginning of the Ages of Chaos. The revised edition of _The Bloody Sun_ (1979) deals with cultural adjustments faced by most Darkovans, but it is also a clearer definition of what being a Darkovan really means. Similarly, "To Keep the Oath," the story published in the same volume as the new _Bloody Sun_, is a Darkovan story, almost entirely independent of Terran influence. _Two to Conquer_ (1980) is a novel of the Ages of Chaos, a further exploration of the old Darkovan ways and doubtlessly evidence of Bradley's unsuccessful dismissal of her planet. _Sharra's Exile_ (1981) may be regarded as a mature author's revision of _The Sword of Aldones_, a novel she clearly regards as inferior. Yet in retelling the story of Lew Alton and the Sharra Rebellion, MZB seems to have carefully "explained" the hold things Darkovan have on her protagonist. Thus, while she brings his story up to date with respect to other Darkover novels set temporally near it, she makes more clear than ever the "reality" of Darkover.

It seems as if she cannot escape it. _Hawkmistress!_ (1982) is another sojourn in the Ages of Chaos that explores both a young woman's coming of age and a special kind of _laran_. _Thendara House_ (1983) is also concerned with _laran_, for the hallucinations shared by Jaelle and Magda indicate not only their emotional relationship but the fact that each of them is struggling through a delayed threshold sickness that accompanies awakening _laran_. And, set in the modern era, _Thendara House_ frequently embodies satirical descriptions of Terran lifeways as Jaelle tries to coexist with everpresent machines. That _Hawkmistress!_ is one of the best of the Darkover novels and that _Thendara House_ is one of the most serious thematically suggest that Bradley, for all her protestations about Terran technology and her science fiction not connected with Darkover at all, has within some region of her mind an attachment to the planet of the bloody sun that even she cannot successfully sever.

Neither can her readers. While it is futile to make inquiries about the satisfactions Bradley attains by bringing into words the essentially Darkovan part of her imagination, one may make the same inquiries as they relate to readers. If life on Darkover is so hard, if its sexist partriarchy is oppressive, if its culture lacks a healthy flexibility, then why is reading about Darkover so rewarding an experience? There are as many answers, probably, as there are readers, but a central one--the real reason for "interest" in reading--is explained by C. S. Lewis:

Those of us who have been true readers all our life seldom fully realise the enormous extension of our

being which we owe to authors....My own eyes are
not enough for me. I will see through those of
others. Reality, even seen through the eyes of
many, is not enough. I will see what others have
invented. Even the eyes of all humanity are not
enough. I regret that the brutes cannot write
books. Very gladly would I learn what face things
present to a mouse or a bee; more gladly still
would I perceive the olfactory world charged with
all the information and emotion it carries for a
dog.
_Literary experience heals the wound, without un-
dermining the privilege, of individuality_...(my
italics). Here, as in worship, in love, in moral
action, and in knowing, I transcend myself; and am
never more myself than when I do. (10)

NOTES

1.   From a telephone interview, July 1980.
2.   Originally, in _Aurora: Beyond Equality_, ed. Vonda
N. McIntyre and Susan Janice Anderson (Greenwich CT: Faw-
cett Publications, Inc., 1976), pp. 132-133; subsequently
reprinted in Le Guin's _The Language of the Night_ and elsewhere.
3.   The reference work is Donald H. Tuck's _Encyclo-
pedia of Science Fiction and Fantasy, Volume I_ (Chicago:
Advent Publishers, 1974). The two novels are listed as part
of the "Darkover Series," yet are described (p. 64) without
specific reference to Darkover.
4.   Private correspondence, February 1980. In the
same letter, Bradley says that she thinks "it, if possible,
worse than _Sword of Aldones_." Her low opinion of the latter
work derives in part from her having published it in haste,
drawing upon fiction written in her teens, to give _The
Planet Savers_ a companion in the 1962 Ace double.
5.   Private correspondence, March 1983.
6.   "XII," lines 17-18, in A. E. Houseman's _Last Poems_
(1922). Probably written in 1900, the poem is most easily
accessible in _The Collected Poems of A. E. Houseman_ (New

York: Henry Holt and Company, 1940), p. 111.

7. The Darkover novels and stories do have a relatively stable internal chronology, but it is impossible to date the settings of each work exactly because of MZB's authorial needs (she adjusts the timing of specific incidents the way she alters the distance between one place and another, subordinating temporal and spatial setting to the whole of each individual work) and because the magnitude of cultural changes on Darkover is simply too great to relegate to the two thousand year interval between the pre-Empire colonizing voyage that ended with the account in _Darkover Landfall_ and the Terran Empire's rediscovery of Darkover. The two thousand years are measured by the Terrans' calendar; at the very beginning of _Sharra's Exile_, Lew Alton suggests that about ten-thousand (Terran) years elapsed on Darkover and that the very nature of time, not being totally understood by anyone anywhere, may account for the discrepancy.

8. Private correspondence, March 1983.

9. Until the publication of _Stormqueen!_ (1978), all the Darkover novels but _Darkover Landfall_ (1972) clearly related to one another within the Darkovan chronology by means of characters who appear in several works and of incidents mentioned as having occurred in the recent past. _The Shattered Chain_ is the first of these. Its temporal setting--soon after Terran Empire ships arrive on Darkover--is clear. It begins what can be called Darkover's "modern era," the time during which MZB's works explore the cultural conflict between Terran and Darkovan ways of life. This modern era is distinct from the Ages of Chaos during which _Stormqueen!_, _Hawkmistress_, and _Two to Conquer_ (in that sequence) are set, for these later novels differ markedly from the others in thematic emphasis.

10. C. S. Lewis, _An Experiment in Criticism_ (Cambridge: Cambridge University Press, 1961), pp. 140-141.

IV

THEMES AND TECHNIQUES: THE SCIENCE FICTION

Bradley began to write when most science fiction was directed at a masculine audience and was peopled almost entirely by protagonists modeled on men. Needless to say, the experience of reading science fiction dominated by a masculine set of interests and the knowledge that men comprised the majority of science-fiction readers were influential. If one wants to be a "real writer"--that is, someone whose works are published and read by others--the gender-orientation of magazines and the men who (for the most part) edited them are very likely to determine that the beginner's first submitted stories will follow the trends set by the stories being bought and published. So Marion Zimmer Bradley's early work may be expected to adhere to the prevailing conventions of the science-fiction-publishing world.

Interestingly, the very first stories she sold took advantage of the relative novelty of a woman's point of view. In "Women Only" (published in Vortex in 1953), the focus of the narration--and the source of its implied conflict and of its interest--is simply the birth of a child. As one reads, one becomes aware that other women characters have strong feelings about this particular childbirth, most of them decidedly negative. The story sets up two questions and then answers them. First, why is the father apparently dismissed as unimportant? Second, why should one woman's bearing a child be the focus of such animosity? By the time the story concludes, the reader relegates the father to the sidelines because he is, after all, only human. And that is the key: somehow, before the temporal setting of the tale, human women were rendered universally sterile while human men were not. The new mother in this story is not, properly, a real human being; she is a genetically altered organism, a creature designed specifically to bear human children and to keep the race from extinction.

With a subtlety that is praiseworthy in a "first story," MZB causes the reader to question the universally positive connotations of motherhood and to question as well the "humanity" of those truly human women who resent a successful childbirth. Has the mutation that caused female infertility rendered fully human females inhuman as well as inhumane? Is the sole function of women reproductive? Has the genetically engineered mother, by virtue of her contribution to the future of the human race and of her very "natural" maternal feelings, become the prototype of the new human woman? Like all good science fiction, the story refuses to answer the questions it raises, but like all good science fiction, it raises some very important ones. Marion Zimmer Bradley got off to a good start.

Her second story, "Keyhole" (published in the same issue of _Vortex_), shows MZB's versatility, commitment to science fiction _per se_, and sensitivity to the market. The viewpoint character, like so many others at that time, is a young man about to make an important scientific breakthrough. The "stranger" who intrudes and causes the conflict in the story is a visitor from the future who, for what may be conventional romantic narrative interest, happens to be a woman. And the basis of the plot is the paradox of "time travel"; to avert the coming-to-be of a "world" destined for catastrophe, the woman from the future must reach the "present" of the story and, necessarily, change history.

The masculine-identification of the story might, with feminist hindsight, be criticized (but then, the choice of the time-traveler's gender would need to be praised, perhaps unduly). Nevertheless, the woman from the future is real enough to evoke readers' credulity and the young man is sufficiently interesting and interested to make the narrative work on the level of interpersonal dynamics. The paradox of "time travel" may, of course, be found to be less than perfectly executed but, for one or two or three readings, it _works_. That MZB, a "new" writer, should take on the challenge of making possible and probable futures not only intelligible as themselves but also understandable in their relation to one another speaks highly of her already-developed familiarity with a commonly attempted yet always difficult science-fiction scenario. That the story does not entangle itself with the myriad potential problems of future-interfering-with-its-past and that the author of the story, from what the story reveals, could be either a woman or a man fairly establishes MZB as a professional writer with a future in science fiction.

"Centaurus Changeling" (F&SF, April 1954), by virtue of its length, the prestigious magazine in which it was published, and its general credibility as a tale of humans among an alien race, has to be regarded as MZB's first really significant work. As "Keyhole" took the matter of time-travel, "Centaurus Changeling" takes xenobiology for its foundation and builds upon that hypothetical yet carefully extrapolated "science" a narrative that is unique and rewarding. The story makes clear MZB's intention to be a science-fiction writer, dealing as it does with the interaction between our own and an alien human race. Like all the stories she published in 1953 and 1954 (with the exception of a serialized version of Falcons of Narabedla that appeared in Harlan Ellison's fanzine), "Centaurus Changeling" is grounded in extrapolation from the sciences we know.

There is, initially, the probability that our descendants will find alien intelligent life "out there" (there is also, common among stories of the same time, an exaggerated "probability" that human-like beings will be found only a few light years away). Then, there is the near-certainty that normal biological processes will be affected by life in a solar system and on a planet different from those of our species' origin. And there is, laudably, the anthropology-influenced belief that the thriving indigenes of any given locality will have customs that help them and that may help us to survive. What is missing is the science-fiction equivalent of "the white man's superiority," and the absence of this attitude in one human character--it is present in other characters in the story for purposes of contrast--makes the story more than just another adventure, although an uncommon one, in "outer space."

"Centaurus Changeling," like MZB's first story, might also have been entitled "Women Only." It, too, focuses on the birth of a human child in unusual, even dangerous circumstances. The plot is simple: since pregnancy on alien worlds is dangerous, it is proscribed for Terran personnel.

The wife of the Terran ambassador, trusting in the gyneco-
logical practices of the native humans, allows herself to
become pregnant and then follows the Centaurus women's example and delivers a healthy Earth-human child. The results
are that she and her husband become emotionally closer, the
Terrans and the Centaurus people become far more trusting of
each other, and the Earth-human infant becomes a real--and
importantly symbolic--ambassador.

Any careful scientific probing into the means by which
the pregnancy is carried to term will, not unexpectedly,
reveal some problematic aspects. The same is true, however,
of most science fiction written during the fifties--a good
story is rarely a detailed scientific treatise, and MZB,
like most of her contemporaries, was intent on producing a
good story. "Centaurus Changeling" makes use of biological
extrapolation to the extent necessary for readers to suspend
their disbelief about the main incident of the plot, but the
focus of the story is not biology or gynecology _per se_. The
focus is human relationships, in this case those between the
Earthmen who decide that Earthwomen cannot risk pregnancy
under certain circumstances and an Earthwoman who is fully
prepared to face the consequences of the risk. Another
focal relationship is the one created by the Earthwoman and
the women who were born beneath another sun. Both these
"human interests" prove to be central to Bradley's career as
a science-fiction writer. Though she pays the necessary
homage to what is scientifically probable, she concentrates
on thematic elements that are less the domain of the physical and natural sciences than they are the province of
what we call today "soft science," the varying offshoots of
the social sciences, such as sociology and psychology.

As a beginning science-fiction writer, Bradley had to
play by the rules: science fiction was supposed to be fiction based on probable results of extrapolation from known
sciences, and thus her earliest published works--most of
them in the form of short stories--are crafted carefully to
avoid blatant violations of what contemporary scientists
said was true or probable. Once she had made a name for
herself, Bradley paid increasing attention to the less certain extrapolations that psychology makes possible. Although Bradley herself feels that anything she wrote earlier
than the mid-sixties is not worth serious consideration,

critics and careful readers are best served by D. H. Lawrence's advice: "Never trust the teller; trust the tale." (1) More recently, Ursula K. Le Guin simultaneously urges the same caution and celebrates disregard for it: "I am an artist, too, and therefore a liar. Distrust everything I say. I am telling the truth." (2) Despite what Bradley says, readers of her early short fiction will find much worth considering quite seriously.

Bradley's progress as a writer had and has the goal of increasingly detailed explorations into human nature. Her earliest published works--the stories mentioned here as well as most that she published within the next several years-- are about "family" in the most profound sense of the word. There is in "Women Only," "Centaurus Changeling," and "Year of the Big Thaw" (1954) an examination of the parent-offspring bond which may fairly be said to define the concept of "family." The first story suggests that a vital aspect of being human inheres in the loving acceptance and nurturance of the being(s) to whom one gives birth. The second suggests that another requisite for humanity is the risk-taking and trust involved in human reproduction, a trust that includes parents and offspring, yes, but that also includes other adults who in various ways make society a macrocosm of the family. And the "Year of the Big Thaw," like "Centaurus Changeling," extends the concept of "family" to persons who are "parents" not only to their own progeny but to the young who may belong to another human (sub)-species.

Her second major published work, "The Climbing Wave" (1955), shows a sensitivity to gender-related uses of language that is at least a decade ahead of its time. More important, the story is an inquiry into a really fundamental aspect of the human condition. The novella is the tale of the descendants of the first interstellar voyage; after much preparation on their dim-lighted homeworld, a group of young people make the triumphant trip back to Earth. They know that their grandparents' mission will be, because of the temporal effects of relativistic travel, mere history. In part because of this, they expect to be welcomed to an Earth that is technologically superior even to their starship's "culture." They are doubly disappointed.

Those pioneers who left Earth for the Centaurus system

are known to the contemporary Earthpeople as "Barbarians"; worse, the inhabitants of Earth use such demeaning expressions as "wife," as if a woman were not the equal of her mate. And, most shocking of all, they find that the homeworld of humanity is scarcely technological at all: the most complicated form of government is the village which, when it grows too large, "fissions" like a protozoon into two smaller ones.

It is important--for literary record-keeping if nothing else--that MZB endows the children of a star-traveling culture with revulsion for sexist-seeming words like "wife" in 1955. It is even more important that the thematic focus of this early novella is the question: "Why should human beings work?"

Twenty-five years later, with the Darkover novels well established as a "text" from which one can draw conclusions about the "technomania" of the Terrans and the "technophobia" of the Darkovans, Bradley was still exploring the same question. In this early novella, though, the question is central and simply but cogently presented. The answer is also simple: human beings should work to ensure the well-being of themselves and of other human beings. The viewpoint character of the novella finds this simple answer difficult to understand and, repeating "the climbing wave" in its original context (the poem "The Lotus Eaters"), thinks that the Earthfolk are like the original lotus eaters of the Odyssey, content to exist placidly and comfortably, without questing after new knowledge or applying current knowledge in novel situations. The Earthfolk in this novella, as far as the viewpoint character can see, have little ambition and even less "scientific curiosity," and he finds these attitudes to be wrong.

MZB has purposely made this character a rigid technocrat so that readers will not identify too strongly with his attitudes, but for the greater part of the novella readers, too, find something lacking in the Earthfolks' very simple lives. There is no technology in evidence! By the conclusion of the narrative, readers and the protagonist discover the technology that does exist and discover too why it is so clearly relegated to a secondary position in the culture. The Earthfolk have electricity, and radio, and airplanes, and almost everything technical that one would want, but

70

they do not build electric generators to have more electricity than they need. Frobisher, one of the leaders of the Earthfolk in his region, explains how, in the "Barbarian Ages," people did not use the radio to talk to one another but instead to entertain, how they kept building things they did not need and then began relying on their unnecessary technology to keep themselves alive. In other words, Frobisher's ancestors were barbarians not because they had an advanced technology but because they allowed technological-- or materialist--values, not human ones, to dominate their lives.

In brief, "The Climbing Wave" presents a utopian vision of the future, in certain respects oversimplified yet over-all--for 1955--an admonitory and entertaining one. People ought not to work, MZB seems to imply, for any other good than that which benefits individual persons. If a family wants a rug and cannot make one, they are best served by locating someone who can make just what they'll like. There is no need for a factory to produce one hundred rugs a day that no one needs or wants. If a sewage-disposal plant for a village is inadequate, it is most unlikely that one that is merely larger will be better. This thematic emphasis on the use of humanity's tools and constructs is not new, but as MZB's authorial habits evolved, increasingly she concentrated on the false progress of material production at the cost of humankind's "spiritual" or non-materialistic values.

In these very early works, MZB begins to explore the themes that become dominant in all her science-fiction and fantasy writing. There is the quest for family, demonstrated by "Women Only" in the genetically-engineered provisions for the future of our species; this same theme is less obviously embodied in the rigid technocrat of "The Climbing Wave," for the young man is lost and is seeking a human group to which he can truly belong. There is also the exploration of the nature of human intimacy--or any sapient intimacy--in "Centaurus Changeling," as the pregnant human woman's behavior strains the relationship between her and her husband and as she comes to know better than any other Earth-human the people on whose homeworld she is to bear her child. All these stories touch upon another of MZB's themes: the meaning of being a woman. As they do, they bring a fourth theme into her literature, since being a

woman is often being a second-class, sometimes not-recog-
nized-as-human, organism: the theme of tolerance. Finally,
as Bradley's career has developed, her fifth major theme--
one might call it a kind of anti-materialism--has emerged
with increasing strength and frequency.

When speaking of her Darkover novels, some readers
complain of the repetition of both theme and summary. The
summary, however repetitious it may seem to a person who has
read most of the Darkover novels and some of them more than
once, must be excused at least partially. The Darkover
novels are not a true series; each of them can stand alone.
For each to be able to stand alone, however, MZB must provide the reader with enough background about Darkover so
that "laran," for instance, will be recognized and not cause
confusion. Thus, the reader well acquainted with Darkover
may silently moan at a clause like "laran, the telepathic
ability that usually emerges during adolescence," but the
reader new to the Darkover fictions will be glad that the
strange new word has been explained.

The more serious objection to Bradley's science fiction
is the charge that it seems to repeat, over and over again,
"thematic statements" in which Bradley herself--or Bradley's
authorial persona--firmly believes. The objection is a
valid one, especially since "theme" is not just a "statement" or, worse, "the moral of the tale," but is instead the
statement into which the reader translates the meanings and
values that are generated by the interaction of the characters and the incidents of the plot and the setting and the
language by which the "whole thing" is communicated.
"Theme" is only part of the "whole thing." Moreover, a
"thematic statement" such as "all women are bound in some
kind of chains, so the wise woman makes sure she chooses the
kind that will bind her" is something that is abstracted
from the "whole thing" that The Shattered Chain is. And the
reader is the one who abstracts such statements.

While it is true that MZB causes incidents and characters to exist in ways that make theme-stating rather easy--
and that she does this is a weakness in her work--it is
nevertheless important to remember that a person who reads
superficially is very likely to oversimplify the themes in
any author's works. Further, when one is dealing with
Bradley, one is dealing with someone who has written very

much. If one counts only her science fiction (remember that she has written much that is not science fiction), there are forty-two books and forty-four stories. Having written that much makes it difficult not to repeat oneself thematically.

There are, then, three "answers" to the charge of too much repetition. One is that, in the Darkover novels, the repetition exists to serve an important purpose. The second is that some readers point and say "repetition!" when actually they should recognize a variation on or a development of some thematic matter present in an earlier work. Third, one must remember that the theme in a novel must be important and as universally significant as possible. Otherwise, allegedly sane persons might spend literally years of their lives writing literature that has for its main thematic statement something like "cats tend to pounce on small moving objects." There are few really important things people can talk about; expunge the trivia and what remains is a lot of silence and a lot of repetition.

The erroneous negative criticisms of Bradley's science fiction aside, there still remain two which have kept her from producing--as a regular activity--works as unflawed as The Mists of Avalon, works that she is obviously capable of writing. The first of these is thematic repetition and the second editorial carelessness. Both derive at least in part from the business of science-fiction writing. Marion Zimmer Bradley has been trying to make a living by writing for twenty-five years. She began her science-fiction career when the standards of the pulp magazines--"tell a good story and forget the other stuff"--still dominated the field. In fact, Jerome Bixby gave Bradley the explicit advice to "stop writing each sentence and phrase with 'style' and get on with your story!" (3) Having had her first experiences with science fiction dominated by tell-the-story requirements and then having the economic facts of life illustrated by how little she could earn from writing a single novel, Bradley developed habits that science fiction would soon outgrow--at least in principle. (4) Marion Zimmer Bradley is nevertheless a major science-fiction writer. Besides having what amounted to her first novel (because she wrote the outline of the plot when she was fifteen), The Sword of Aldones, come very close to winning a Hugo Award, many of her later works have been Nebula or Hugo contenders. The World

<u>Wreckers</u> (1971), <u>Darkover Landfall</u> (1972), <u>The Heritage of Hastur</u> (1975), <u>The Shattered Chain</u> (1976), "Hero's Moon," (1976), and <u>The Forbidden Tower</u> (1977) were all nominated for Nebula Awards. <u>The Heritage of Hastur</u> was on the final ballot, <u>The Forbidden Tower</u> outranked all but the winner in the Hugo balloting that year, and <u>StormQueen!</u> (1978) earned an honorable mention in the voting for the Hugo Award. In the 1979 Hugo voting, Bradley placed fifth for the "Grand Master of Fantasy (Gandalf) Award." Whenever a new book of hers is released, it almost immediately finds a high place on the list of science-fiction bestsellers. Coincidence or luck cannot account for all of this.

At her best, MZB uses language exquisitely; her two latest fantasies and a surprising number of her early stories are evidence. At her worst, MZB still produces science-fiction narratives that sell well enough to be sought after, bought, and even reprinted. The most serious problem with MZB's science fiction is that the authorial persona lacks a "best friend," a persona endowed with sufficiently obsessive-compulsive qualities for it to function as grammarian, copy-editor, and proofreader. Bradley's most probable response to this statement is something to the effect that she is a writer, not a copy-editor, and let the copy-editors do their jobs. Unfortunately, most copy-editors know less of English syntax, style, and punctuation than Bradley does. Equally unfortunately, most readers do not notice a somewhat run-on sentence here and a textual inconsistency (for instance, the same character in the same novel during the same interval using first a depilatory cream on his beard and then complaining about his razor), <u>and</u> <u>publishers</u> <u>know</u> both these unfortunate facts. "Leave well enough alone; it sells" is all too true.

The question that arises from "it sells" is almost obvious: what is it about MZB's science fiction that engages the interest of readers who, despite their awareness of the carelessness with language, continue to read and then reread her books? What is it about her science fiction that enables some--probably most--readers of her works never to notice the stylistic infelicities and, sometimes, outright mistakes? The answer easiest to put in words is "Bradley's sense of wonder."

Marion Zimmer Bradley is a science-fiction fan. She

has held on to a naivete that lets her see the universe around her with an attitude that is the opposite of cynicism. She has certainly lived long enough to know the nasty side of things, and she has undoubtedly been hurt more times than she would care to count. Not as an escape but as transcendence, she takes her innocent self and thrusts it into the persona known as MZB and then lets MZB tell stories. The stories, whether short or novel-length, look out upon the universes they call into being with a bias, and the bias can be rendered fairly as "All things considered, everything's okay." Leigh Brackett, friend of Marion Zimmer Bradley, once described the appeal of science fiction:

> These stories served to stretch our little minds, to draw us out beyond our narrow skies into the vast glooms of interstellar space, where the great suns ride in splendor and the bright nebulae fling their veils of fire parsecs-long across the universe; where the Coal-sack and the Horsehead make patterns of black mystery; where the Cepheid variables blink their evil eyes and a billion nameless planets may harbor life-forms infinitely numerous and strange. (5)

To this paean Marion Zimmer Bradley, as herself or as MZB, might add "and where we can become our truest selves."

In Endless Voyage, later revised and expanded into Endless Universe (1975, 1979), MZB presents the family-like Explorers, members of a starship's crew. They travel slowly, at lightspeed, finding new worlds upon which humanity can make yet another home; they set up the Transmitter booths, so that the planet-dwellers can travel almost instantaneously from world to world. Their hair and skin is bleached by stellar radiation, and they are sterile, for they've spent too much "objective" time in space. Even "subjectively," they live long lives; as real old age approaches, they more or less "retire" to the parts of the ship where gravity is hardly felt.

But, for all they do to give more worlds to others, they are outcasts, needing to buy (or sometimes steal) infants to keep the "family-crew" from dying out. In telling of the adventures of one such crew of Explorers, MZB examines on a large scale what "family" and "love" and "intimacy" mean. The whole ship is the home, the crew the family; each member shares the all-important task of guiding unrelated infants through childhood and adolescence so that, when they mature, the new crew members know the love that gives them the security to take their places as skilled, responsible, and family-oriented adults.

In several places where new material made Endless Voyage into Endless Universe, "the seams show." For example, a character refers to an incident in the near past as if it happened fairly recently when, in the revised text, a novella-length adventure has taken place between the incident and the reference to it. If one cares for exactitude, Endless Universe contains some awkward errors. If one cares for verbal rendering of what love, loyalty, family, and other important values are, Endless Universe is more than satisfactory. It is not a masterpiece, but it will do.

It will do what every piece of real literature achieves: it puts into words, which describe minutely, concrete things and characters with a psychological and emotional ambiance that people who are not literary artists respond to by saying "Yes, that's exactly it. I couldn't put it into words, but here it is." A more sophisticated reader can find in Endless Universe a careful use of metaphor and symbol. The ship is, of course, a macrocosmic family; its crew is bound together not by rules or levels of command but by love. The ship is also suggestive of a well-integrated, selfless person: it travels through the glooms of space, each person in it knowing that anyone he or she knew on any planet is very likely to be dead before that planet is visited again. Yet the ship and its crew continue, directed by a voluntary responsibility to open up new worlds for humankind.

The ship and its crew are also, obviously, a microcosmic society, even a microcosmic world. Self-contained and isolated by the immensities of galactic and intergalactic space from other groups of people, the crew does its work, motivated by a familial-social love. MZB does not offer her readers only an idealistic picture, for the joys are balanced if not outweighed by the lonely, tearing griefs. The balance is dynamic; it makes the novel interesting. But somehow, in describing the particularities of griefs and joys, MZB endows the book with an optimism that is not shallow. Her themes may not be original, but they are good: the reader is left feeling better about humanity after having read. We do not need "the seams that show," but we cannot do without the kind of experience novels like this one give us. One might correct the placement of some sentences, but one cannot easily--or with great difficulty-- improve upon the warm, familial humanity that Endless Universe portrays.

If Endless Universe offers to its readers a sense of home, of family-that-is-the-world, of love-that-is-a-quiet- ground-on-which-to-stand, then, Hunters of the Red Moon (1973) shows with electrifying vigor the passion that the threat of death evokes from camaraderie and love. This novel is space opera, a fast-paced narrative of adventure that slows down only long enough--in breaks between the action--to raise thematic issues seldom connected with stories that have fight-or-die kinds of plots. The most arresting device by which MZB explores the nature of in- timacy in Hunters is the character of Dallith, an empath from Spica Four. A captive, like the Earthman Dane Marsh and the other major characters, Dallith is ready to suicide, for members of her race are not only keenly sensitive to those around them but almost helpless, psychically, without the company of their own species.

Dane, the jaded adventurer from an over-civilized Earth, comes into contact with the others after cat-like beings take him from his one-man yacht into their flying saucer. Sensitive hero that he is, Marsh finds Dallith letting herself die and stops her--feeds her, stays by her-- motivated unconsciously by his own need to have impact. An empath, Dallith--and, in time, the reader--realizes that Marsh's act of heroism is really just a sign of his need to have some function in his environement. So emotionally needy is this Earthman hero that the empath woman delays her very death for him.

This description makes the novel seem trite and formu- laic; in many ways, it is. There is a not-too-original plot; a predictable protagonist; his wise, brave, trusting friend; and two human women whom the hero loves; and danger, their deathly peril as Sacred Prey on the Red Moon. But MZB pulls it off: Hunters is a gripping adventure story that also celebrates human relationships closer than sexual ones and that allows death to take the one chief character who, because of her pain and courage, should survive. Almost from the beginning of the narrative and almost to the end, Dane Marsh finds himself in love with two women at the same time. MZB makes use of this stock situation by showing how the sexual relationship Dane has with Rianna is equalled if not surpassed in intimacy by the less carnal love he shares with Dallith.

And then there is Aratak, a huge saurian philosopher with whom Dane shares another kind of love--or is it so different from the love he feels for Dallith? (The question suggests that all three "loves" are basically the same.) The delicacy with which these relationships are treated seems out of place in a book the central superficial quality of which is the fight for survival on an alien world. The delicacy of Marsh's feelings for Dallith and the strange ambivalence Marsh feels about the sexual way in which he and Rianna are able to relate contrast vividly with the superb adventure scenes, as the adventures make us more aware of the emotional and psychological growth of the protagonist.

Then, more: Aratak may be an imposing fighter when he is roused, but when he is presented as himself, his quotations of the Divine Egg give the novel yet another dimension, humor. In The Survivors (1979), Aratak's quotations are made farcical, and both his character and that novel suffer. But in Hunters, MZB integrates Paul Edwin Zimmer's knowledge of the martial arts, her own sensitive portrayals of an empath and a man learning about the different ways of loving, plotting that is paced almost perfectly, humor that is really funny, and space-opera adventure into a work requiring several readings to do it justice.

To survey Marion Zimmer Bradley's science fiction is to see great variety as well as to notice the recurrence of several basic themes. Some of her early stories--"Jackie Sees a Star" (1954) for instance--are limited; reading them now, we note that they were "good for their time." Yet other work of hers is not so easy to dismiss--as "Jackie Sees a Star" is not if thought of as an upbeat analogue of Judith Merril's "That Only a Mother" (1948). "Measureless to Man" (1962) could be inserted into Leigh Brackett's The Coming of the Terrans (stories written between 1948 and

1964) and, if a reader were not really familiar with the work of Bradley and Brackett (both greatly influenced by C. L. Moore), he or she would be hard put to tell which is Bradley's and which is Brackett's Mars. Bradley acknowledges her debt to Brackett's The Starmen (of Llyrdis) (1952) for the "germ" of her own The Colors of Space (1963) but, if anything, Bradley's novel seems the better one. (6)

The variety in Bradley's works can be attributed to her psychological situation (she needs to write; she likes to write) and to her resolute sense of wonder. Having read Brackett's Starmen, for example, Marion Zimmer Bradley might well have said: "Now, that's an idea; but what if all the human races could endure interstellar flight? That's much more democratic, fairer..." and MZB would soon be directing the telling of what came to be The Colors of Space. A little later, Bradley would read another novel or story. Depending on the circumstances, not one but several stories could result from just one source. This psychogenetic guessing about what moves MZB to write such different stories is hypothetical, although the explanation of The Colors in Space is grounded in the truth. And from it comes a problem: so much to write, so little time.

One of Bradley's responses to this problem has been a sharing of the Darkover setting and even characters with fans who want to write about them. The two anthologies, The Keeper's Price and Other Stories (1980) and Sword of Chaos (1982), are the results. They, and the 1983 Greyhaven anthology of fantasy stories, have been the object of some minor controversy. "It's going a bit too far to let them use her characters," one MZB admirer might say. "And to put her name on all that stuff!" might be another person's moan. Yet still another answer: "But Wollheim's publishing them, and not just as a hobby," for the truth is that these anthologies are bought. And read. And, if one applies to them "Sturgeon's Law" (that 90% of anything that's published is, to put it nicely, trash), the anthologies hold up. If they did not, detractors might find satisfaction but little else: the "Friends of Darkover" anthologies exist because Marion Zimmer Bradley, that grown-up successful fan, has helped them to exist. Finis.

Tangentially related to the matter of Darkover anthologies is the fact that, no matter what else happens in a given year, Marion Zimmer Bradley will get another Darkover novel done. Until the recent Thendara House was published in 1983, it seemed as if MZB had done all there was to do with Darkover in the "modern era"; in fact, one criticism of this recent novel is that, unlike most others, it does not stand solidly alone. It is a sequel to The Shattered Chain in a way that The Forbidden Tower is not a sequel to the earlier Spell Sword. Because it promises another novel that will make it and The Shattered Chain a trilogy about the Free Amazons, this criticism is not a strong one. City of Sorcery (1984) became the third book in Jaelle's "trilogy," but the end of Magda's and Camilla's adventures remains untold. One thing is certain: the Darkover novels keep coming.

Even with the publication of Thendara House and City of Sorcery, the more recent fiction set on Darkover has set a thematic course and made use of authorial techniques that are clearly related to all of Bradley's science fiction. One technique may mirror the demands of the marketplace: there is decidedly more sexual activity presented as "scene" than in the past. In Survey Ship (1980), a work not set in any of MZB's already-created universes and a work aimed directly at the "young adult" fiction market, characters' sexual preferences and activities seem to be the objects of most of MZB's attention. In Thendara House, Magda's chief adjustments to the ways of the Renunciates appear as Magda's trying out new sexual experiences, and in City of Sorcery, the reader learns in detail of the difference between Magda's love for Jaelle (her freemate) and for Camilla (her lover). The use of sex as metaphor and symbol appears to be a minor shift--minor because MZB has always dealt with sexuality--in MZB's technique.

But, especially in Thendara House, the use of the sexual act as symbolic of the most intimate kind of sharing may seem a fail-safe rather than a sign of authorial control. In The Forbidden Tower, the more-than-physical intimacy of four telepaths is rendered well by the inadequacy of sexual contact to communicate all that the four want to share. In The Forbidden Tower, MZB's use of sexual contact as metaphor for the deepest kind of interpersonal intimacy works. In Thendara House, unless one interpolates significance from previous novels, Magda's afternoon with Monty--

especially since it precedes her initial lovemaking with Camilla later the same day--seems precipitate if not promiscuous. On the other hand, if one regards Thendara House as a work dependent on The Shattered Chain, one may regard Magda's sudden sexual excursions as desperate attempts to bind herself intimately with one world (Camilla's Darkover) or the other (Monty's Terran Zone). Either way, sex-as-symbol is thematically fitting.

It may, however, be too easy to use, too powerful a symbol for frequent appearances in a novel: thematic impact may be inversely proportional to frequency within a single work of literature. In this context--the too-hasty use of a powerful symbol for thematic effect--the sexuality portrayed by MZB may be defeating its own purposes. If it is, then, the state of the market (MZB has characters in Survey Ship use language that Bradley herself finds truly offensive) and Bradley's need to get all of it into words as quickly and as fully as possible are working together against Bradley-the-artist's best interests.

One of Bradley-the-artist's sustained thematic interests has been the role of technology, not just on Darkover but in all her science-fiction settings. One might say that, for some, "the machine" is as thematically meaningful in MZB's work as the acts of sexual intimacy are. If one regards the Darkover fictions as a kind of standard, one can notice, with MZB's forays into the Ages of Chaos, a subtle shifting of thematic emphasis. Thendara House and City of Sorcery are proof that the modern era has not yet been fully exploited, but, accustomed to think about the Darkover novels as treatments of the conflicting values held by the non-industrial Darkovans and the technomaniacal Terran Empire, one may wonder what attraction leads MZB toward the Ages of Chaos. Looking at very recently published works-- two fantasies in which magic has as solid an existence as the characters themselves--one may wonder what the magic "means."

The Darkover novels offer the clearest suggestions. Without the Terran presence, there is no mechanical technology on the planet. There is, during the Ages of Chaos, misuse of Laran that has the same effects as mechanically-contrived hard radiation and napalm and other horrors more usually associated with technology, but the Compact evolves in response to it. Without misuse of <u>Laran</u>, pre-modern Darkover has a technology without a materialist philosophy on which to base it. The human psyche, not any machine, empowers a technology that is ideal (and, for that matter, hypothetical, at least on the Darkover we can read about). Along with the exploration of a non-materialist technology, MZB's treatment of the Free Amazons is most significant. During the modern era, <u>they</u> call themselves Renunciates, but even MZB in her earlier works calls them Amazons. In <u>Two</u> <u>to</u> <u>Conquer</u> (1980), however, we learn of the history of the group: the "sisters of the sword" joined the priestess-healers of Avarra. In early modern times, the chief authority of the Thendara Guild House is called <u>Mother</u> Lauria. Little by little, MZB is remaking the history of mercenaries like Kindra so that she, for one example, is analogous to a member of "the church militant." Or, in simplistic terms, the Renunciates of Darkover are being stripped of materialism to be endowed with a secular spirituality.

Thus, as the past of Darkover is explored in more detail, the Amazons become more insistently identified as the Order of Renunciates. As the early misuse of <u>laran</u> is described as horrible, its proper use becomes defined as a non-mechanical way to raise the level of a civilization. Free women become spiritual sisters, and civilization depends on (at least vaguely) "spiritual" power. As MZB reworks one of her earliest books, the narrative focus is spiritual: priests and priestesses (of differing persuasions) are the major characters, and the fate of the civilization of Atlantis depends on an act of profanation. In <u>The</u> <u>Mists</u> <u>of</u> <u>Avalon</u>, Morgaine, more commonly known as Morgan le Fay, does not commit incest because her union with the King Stag is a sacred rite. Or, if her and Arthur's union was incestuous, Morgaine's intercession (as priestess at the time of his death) saved both of them from the otherworldly consequences of their sin.

Marion Zimmer Bradley is a writer of science fiction, but the "science" that has been first among her interests is <u>the</u> "science" of "truth," that "truth of the human heart." (7)

Bradley writes science fiction because she must, and she must because she loves it. To her and to readers aware of the technocracy around them, the "rules of science" or

"natural laws" are of greatest interest and importance as
they apply to the human being. Moving away from her early
extrapolations from biology, and then even from psychology,
Bradley has nevertheless been speculating about the "laws"
that make an organism with a big brain a living human being.
She has, for the past several years at least, been studying
that most ancient of human sciences, the codified knowledge
of elemental forces in their interrelations with humanity;
she has been writing from an increasing knowledge of ancient
and modern magic and religious truth. She has explored the
rules of the psyche or soul in her fantasies; we must look
to Darkover and elsewhere to see how she will extrapolate
from them in her science fiction.

NOTES

    1. D. H. Lawrence, "The Spirit of Place," in Studies
in Classic American Literature (1923) Reprinted, New York:
The Viking Press, 1961), p. 2.
    2. "Introduction" to Ursula K. Le Guin, The Left Hand
of Darkness (New York: Ace Books, reprintings of 1976 and
thereafter), p. xii.
    3. Paraphrased; at a writing workshop Bradley conduc-
ted in November 1980.
    4. Science fiction is not alone in the "business" of
rewarding quantity instead of quality; publishing anything
except blockbuster bestsellers simply doesn't pay. A first-
novel author is still likely to be advanced only $2,000 or
so against royalties of 6 to 8% of the original paperback's
gross sales of the first 100,000 copies (and to sell 100,000
copies is bestseller activity, very rare indeed). One sad
way to regard the "business" is to remember that, in many
states, a buyer pays as sales tax just about exactly what
the author earns as royalties.
    5. Leigh Brackett, "Introduction," The Best of Planet
Stories #1 (New York: Ballantine Books, 1975), p. 3.
    6. The comparison of these novels is fair, since each
was written about a decade after its author made her professional debut. That Bradley had Brackett's work to react to
is balanced by the fact that Brackett's novel was expanded

from her 1951 novelette.

    7. In Nathaniel Hawthorne's preface to <u>The</u> <u>House</u> <u>of</u> <u>the</u> <u>Seven</u> <u>Gables</u> (1851), third sentence of the second paragraph; so cited because of the innumerable editions in which the quotation appears.

V.

THE FANTASIES

Marion Zimmer Bradley does not, typically, write fantasy. During the course of her long career (with the exception of _Falcons of Narabedla_, a "shameless imitation of C. L. Moore and Henry Kuttner" which she would unpublish if she could), (1) she has been careful to extrapolate the basis of her fictions from contemporary science and technology. Very early, the science was biology and her stories were notable because they introduced the "idea" that science-fiction characters come in two genders. As her career developed, she adopted masculine as well as feminine viewpoints in her narratives, and her extrapolations began to veer away from biology itself toward psychology and then toward the less respectable knowledge of paranormal sensory activity.

At the very beginning of her career--before she had had anything published and before she had left her teens--Marion Zimmer Bradley's chosen genre was fantasy. She liked to play with characters with psionic talents; she did not shy away from magic; and, interestingly, her most ambitious pre-professional fantasy was built around the actions of two characters who are feminine in gender. Thus, while Bradley earned her reputation writing science fiction, she is no stranger to the fantastic. And, as her explorations of Darkover grew in detail, her concentration on "psi"--less sympathetically called "magic"--moved the main body of her writing into the realm called science fantasy.

This chapter treats four true fantasies: _Web of Light_, _Web of Darkness_, _The House Between the Worlds_, and _The Mists of Avalon_. The first two are really the same work, made into two volumes because one would be too long and because the narratives lend themselves to a tidy division. (2) These fantasies date to the very beginnings of Bradley's career, actually to that time before she published anything professionally, that time when she was--probably unconsciously--putting into her mind all sorts of information that would later emerge as fiction.

What is primarily notable about the Web novels is a paradoxical relationship among the usual elements of works of fiction: the plot, characters, setting, theme, and prose style. Because this fantasy has been thoroughly rewritten at least four times, because it has had the advantages of Bradley's elder son's preparation of the final draft and editorial attention of David Hartwell (former science-fiction editor for Pocket Books), and because it is essentially the work of an amateur written by a professional, its smoothness of style seems nearly out of place among characters that fall just short of being convincing.

Unless one has already read The Mists of Avalon (the final draft of which was also prepared by her elder son, David Bradley), one is almost surprised by the simple beauty of the prose in the Web novels. In most of her recent fiction, MZB's use of language is pleasantly unnoticeable; the style seems transparent, keeping the reader in touch with what "the story" is but for the most part keeping the reader unaware of the precise manner in which the language is being used. In the Web fantasy, by contrast, one does not rush through the narrative to find out how things will be resolved but instead pauses and repeats mentally (or even aloud) a phrase or sentence that is striking for its rhythm or other aural quality.

Readers who have read The Mists of Avalon but no other works by Bradley, readers impressed with the way Mists is written and curious to find other of this author's works, may--because Web of Light was published shortly after the other, longer work--pick up a copy of the Timescape paperback and conclude that they've discovered an author who merits more attention. They will reach this conclusion because of the prose style. Such readers will find it difficult indeed to believe that the Web fantasy was first written more than thirty years ago. If they are the sort of readers who categorize authors whose works they've read, they'll file "Marion Zimmer Bradley" away safely in the place marked "Fine Prose Stylist." They'll be correct.

Other readers, familiar with earlier works by Bradley, will find in the Web novels reason for quiet celebration. "Finally," they may say to themselves, "finally, she has

taken care with the language of her fiction that her fiction
has long deserved." They'll be right, too.

After finishing Web of Light, however, these happy
readers may feel a bit mystified. When they finish Web of
Darkness, they may feel somewhat let down. Here are two
good fantasy novels, written beautifully, with plots that
are resolved satisfactorily and characters that are neither
inconsistent nor unduly shallow. The novels "work" but--
this is the sign of their actual age--they do not linger in
the reader's mind. Somehow, these novels do not make magni-
ficent the central incident about which they revolve: they
are a telling of the demise of the civilization of Atlantis
and, as far as plotting goes, they tell the tale as well as
one might want, but there is no sense of apocalyptic gran-
deur that ought to go along with the end of a great and
ancient culture. "So that's why Atlantis sank. Oh."

This is not to say that these two novels are not worth
reading. They are. They are better than at least eighty-
five percent of what is currently being published as fantasy. They are the work of a mature writer. They bear
evidence of Bradley's scholarship: they make a world and a
way of life consistent and, within their boundaries, believable. The problem is they are not "great." That they
have been published so recently--and so long after their
original conception--gives them the advantage of being so
well written that even a careful reader will not look for
flaws until he or she has finished reading both Web books.
But that they are, in essence, the fruit of the imagination
of a college student makes them fall short of the marks set
by the serious thematic probing of the more recent Darkover
novels and by The Mists of Avalon, a work that puts whatever
one compares with it into an unflattering if not unfavorable
light.

The House Between the Worlds is and is not uncharac-
teristic of MZB's usual authorial procedure. In the dedication to Poul Anderson, Bradley thanks the other author for
introducing her to the world of the Alfar and for letting
her know that that world is not a personally invented one
but instead a part of the "Commonwealth of Literature." (3)
There is not the least bit of levity or exaggeration in the
dedication. For Marion Zimmer Bradley, the "Commonwealth of
Literature" is real, an entity with many regions, a cosmos

to be explored with respect. The "world of the Alfar" is what most of us would call "faery-land"; and, calling it that, we would be making a definitive statement: it is the place or realm (or whatever word is best) where the faery dwell--not gnomes and hobbits and other sorts of fantasy creatures, just the faery. In her recent <u>Dreamstone</u>, C. J. Cherryh creates another window that self-consciously opens into that same world. (4) Hobbits, or course, belong in Middle Earth, another realm or plane or dimension, and only foolish rationalists who do not believe in their reality would look for them elsewhere. Fantasy has laws.

The strict adherence to these laws--like her very early science fiction, which grew out of extrapolation from the scientific disciplines--is one of the aspects of <u>The House Between the Worlds</u> that has puzzled many readers. If one is used to the Darkover novels, for instance, in which MZB bends a few rules or laws to enhance her stories, one is not quite prepared for the strictness of her extrapolations in this fantasy novel. First, there is an uncanny verisimilitude about the way that the Berkeley campus and its vicinity are portrayed: no, the real and fictional Berkeleys are not identical, but yes, one can almost point to the storefront on the real Telegraph Avenue that sometimes becomes the Worldhouse. (5) Second, similarly, the fictional Berkeley is not at all "unreal" in other respects; the cyclic repetition of students' lifestyles just may find "hippies" and "street people" behaving, in fifteen or twenty years, the way that MZB depicts the minor characters in this novel.

A second kind of strictness is evident in the creation of a "Department of Parapsychology": were such a department to exist, it <u>would</u> be running experiments with ESP cards after the example of Rhine at Duke, and it <u>would</u> be collectively paranoid and bitter about the skepticism and open disbelief with which the results of any of its many-times-replicated experiments would be greeted. In setting up this narrative, MZB is careful to follow trends realistically. People have always been--at least in the mainstream of Western culture--all too ready to deny the evidence of their own senses if that evidence points toward the validity of hypotheses about the existence of paranormal human mental processes. One of the difficulties the novel poses may come, perhaps, from the fact that Marion Zimmer Bradley

herself is not at all a skeptic about "ESP"; she is convinced of the reality of paranormal abilities and will not
waste time arguing with someone who considers them impossible. In contrast, her fictional department of parapsychology seems to have been created by an "author" who is willing to argue, by an authorial voice that keeps reminding
readers to keep their minds open to the possibility of
parapsychological phenomena. To keep from violating its own
advice about keeping one's mind open, this voice makes every
effort to be very careful about "following the rules." The
persona that narrates this novel is clearly distinct from
Bradley herself.

The third kind of strictness--probably the one that
makes more readers feel uneasy than the other two--in The
House Between the Worlds is an almost absolute adherence to
the "laws" of fantasy. At this point, the word "fantasy" is
too inexact to be used without qualification. Here, we are
dealing with two kinds of fantasy: one is a psychological
process, and the other is a literary form. Both have
"rules" that cannot be put aside.

As a psychological phenomenon, fantasy is what happens
when a person's mind, in a waking state, functions the way
it does while the person dreams. In his Biographia Liter-
aria, Coleridge makes an important distinction between imagination and fancy. Imagination, he says, is the aspect of
the mind that synthesizes something new from its stores of
what it has experienced, while fancy merely joins two not-
new phenomena which the mind has experienced. The common
conception of a mermaid--a being with a woman's body except
that the hips, legs, and feet are replaced by the posterior
half of a fish (woman + fish = mermaid)--is the result of
fancy. By contrast, the character Geraldine is a product of
imagination: there are about her aspects of the vampire,
the lesbian seductress, the old hag or witch, the serpent
that paralyzes its prey by its gaze, the innocent maiden in
distress, the beautiful woman who uses her charms to attract
men, and more. Geraldine of Coleridge's poem "Christabel"
is more than the sum of the parts here listed; Geraldine is
as original (and at the same time as familiar-seeming) as a
creature from a dream or nightmare. Geraldine is a creature
of fantasy.

It does not really matter which psychological approach

is used to explain how the mind, in its dreaming state, functions. What MZB's parapsychologists complain of--that the not-conscious, not-rational workings of the mind have not been sufficiently explored--is fact as well as fiction. Despite other differences, all psychological "schools" are insistent about the "fact" that the sub- or unconscious mind works not chaotically but according to immutable rules. One such rule is that a dream will recur until its content has somehow been assimilated by the waking mind. Another is that a dream-action, which the conscious mind will not ("cannot") remember, is analogous to an intention--say, to act out a revenge--which the conscious mind "censors" and of which, thereby, the conscious mind is unaware. If the act/intention is strong enough and if the consciousness succeeds in remaining unaware of it, then (here is the "rule") some apparently unrelated symptomatic behavior will occur. The behavior may be called a phobia, or it may take the form of an ulcer, or it may appear as a facial tic. How it manifests itself is unimportant compared to the importance of "obeying the rule" by somehow confronting whatever is repressed. There are other rules, as well, which we obey whether or not we are aware of obeying them; when we catch ourselves thinking of tripping the person upon whom we (do not know we) want revenge, we are catching ourselves in an act of fantasy.

"Daydreaming" is another manifestation of psychological fantasy. At times, one "catches oneself" and discovers that, for the past several minutes, one has been "in another world," doing something far more pleasant or interesting than whatever ordinary tasks one has neglected. At other times, a person does not need a sudden self-discovery because the person knows that he or she is daydreaming and voluntarily continues the "dream" to its pleasant conclusion. The way things happen in a daydream and the way they happen during sleep follow the same rules. Unfortunately, thinking that rationality or consciousness is somehow better than intuition or dream has made it extremely difficult to learn about these rules while conscious. And when we are not conscious, we may learn about these rules but, obviously, we'll be unaware of what we've learned.

...Unless, however, we take literary fantasy seriously. What is called "high fantasy" conforms most closely with those not-quite-known rules of psychological fantasy. In Tolkien's _Lord of the Rings_ trilogy, Sauron and his minions are defeated, but not without terrible cost. As we read the trilogy, we sense that something is "right" about the way things happen. We sorrowfully agree with Elrond that the great war will have a permanent and bad effect upon the world even if the war is won. We do not know _why_ we know that Elrond is right, nor do we know exactly _why_ the narrative is so engrossing--at least, we do not know why _consciously_. Therein lies at least one reason for the satisfaction that literary fantasy gives: it tells of unreal things and persons and events if we read it only at the most literal level, but, because we _cannot_ read it only at that level--because the fantasy we read resonates inside our psyches and speaks directly to what we call the sub- or unconscious mind--literary fantasy is, like no other form of literature, deeply and thoroughly satisfying.

It very well may be that the psychic "setting" of a fantasy determines its special nature. C. J. Cherryh's _Dreamstone_, because it takes place in only two worlds, is a convenient example. The "real world" in the narrative exists on the plane or in the realm of "heroic fantasy," which is a kind of epic literature that celebrates the valor of its warrior-heroes whose actions take place in a world that is similar to our own during the barbarian invasions of Europe and the following Middle Ages. The world of faery, on the other hand, is one of the places where "high fantasy" can occur. In Cherryh's novel, the world of faery and that of humankind are drifting apart but are tangent at several important points. Time in faery, for example, does not pass with nearly the rapidity that marks our own world's years and seasons. Thus, the faery themselves do not seem to age, and the humans they allow inside their realm, upon leaving it, find themselves strangely younger than their former contemporaries are. In faery, everything seems predestined (as it is in "high fantasy"), while in a semi-real "heroic" past, the champion or hero can and usually does affect the turn of events.

The Lord of the Rings is high fantasy. More than an account of the battle between good and evil, it is the story of the last days of Middle Earth, when the elves--like the Alfar, like the faery--depart from _this_ world because the

time of humankind has arrived. In <u>The</u> <u>Dreamstone</u>, one of
the faery returns; in <u>Lord</u> <u>of</u> <u>the</u> <u>Rings</u>, not all of the
elvin folk have departed. Both works depend heavily upon a
"world"--or a part of one--that has not yet wholly changed;
both depend heavily on the interaction between the older
Folk and the upstart race that is humanity. And so does <u>The</u>
<u>House</u> <u>Between</u> <u>the</u> <u>Worlds</u>.

Some people need recourse to a psychology that admits
of a "collective unconscious" to explain both the deep
satisfaction derived from reading high fantasy and the sense
that certain realms or planes of reality have existence
apart from a single individual person's experience of them.
Both dreams and high fantasy produce uncanny intuitions of
<u>deja</u> <u>vu</u>: the sense that Middle Earth or the world of the
Alfar would exist even if one never read about them, the
wonder that another person has, in her or his dreaming,
envisioned or experienced something ordinarily thought to be
absolutely individual. Jungian psychology, for instance,
easily explains how reading or dreaming about the iron-folk,
say, may be new to the reader or dreamer but not new at all
to the collective human mind.

One does not require any such structure to account for
the temporal discrepancies between our own world and any of
the others, however. The distortion of time-sense is evident in the most ordinary dreams. They may seem, experien-
tially, to take hours, while the heightened nervous activity
that is a dream may last, really, only a few moments. When
a person is influenced by any consciousness-altering drug,
similarly, the passage of time as it is "experienced" often
differs markedly from what an "objective" clock records.
Thus, Fenton quite realistically cannot judge time when he
is a visitor in any of the planes of worlds that his use of
the fictional drug Antaril causes him to visit.

<u>The</u> <u>House</u> <u>Between</u> <u>the</u> <u>Worlds</u> is a somewhat unsettling
book primarily because MZB uses the techniques of careful
extrapolation in a fantasy. She makes use of her knowledge
of magic, comparative religion, and cultural anthropology
just as "hard" science-fiction writers use geophysics to
construct planets on which to set their narratives. MZB
takes a "natural law" of dream and fantasy--the "law" that
permits free association to bind two dissimilar experiences,
so that when one thinks of one, the other is evoked--and

makes it work as surely as the law of gravitation. She makes use of legend and magic in the same way: a "gate" between worlds may open only at full moon; almost all "worlds" are tangent to one another at the equinoxes and solstices. Her use of these conventions is authoritative.

Most readers will raise an eyebrow at the howling of dogs at a full moon because most readers live where dogs are kept indoors at night. They are probably unaware of the function of howling in a wolf pack--dogs are the descendents of domesticated wolves--and the hunting advantages conferred on wolves and other predators by the full moon. (6) Persons who staff mental health facilities know all too well that "lunatic" has a specific meaning and that suicide attempts and the winter solstice correlate too well to be explained away as coincidence. Thus, it may well be that Pentarn's use of "patches" instead of true gates is controlled "free" association. Since the world he rules is a fascist one, such control of what is normally spontaneous is at the least consistent. Strengthened magic at equinox or solstice has if anything more validity, for these are the times when the axial tilt of the planet is most noticeable: at each equinox, the Earth's axis is perpendicular to the plane of its orbit, and the solstices mark those times when the plane of the axis makes the most acute angle with the orbital plane. At each of these four times, the Earth's axis is for an instant statis with respect to its orbit around the sun; the (magic?) statis can explain very well why our world is "open to" the others.

In The House Between the Worlds, MZB accomplishes much more than is at first apparent. She sets up a fairly ordinary plot--the "lost" character finds himself and a woman he can truly love after many difficulties--and then loads it with material gathered from both fantasy and science fiction. Unlike Simak's Fellowship of the Talisman, in which fairly standard fantasy hides the true science fiction until very near the conclusion, The House Between the Worlds uses the conventions of science fiction to validate the fantasy. The novel presents fantasy as fantasy and then, not only thematically but by means of character and other literary elements, argues that the fantastic elements are as real as Telegraph Avenue is in Berkeley.

In Coleridge's terms, the novel as a whole is the

product of imagination, not fancy. What is unfortunate is that, working within the established rules for fantasy, MZB makes use of fancy to bind some of the incidents to the novel. It may be that this cannot be helped in so experimental a work of fantasy. And, even with its shortcomings, The House Between the Worlds renders the Alfar as "true" and the gnome and his world as real evidence of the literary imagination at work. The same cannot be said of the Web fantasy, for if one compares it with The House Between the Worlds, it becomes apparent that the characters in the very early fantasy are the result less of imagination than fancy.

The Mists of Avalon is Bradley's masterpiece. Although it is a retelling of the Arthurian legend and is grounded soundly in historical and literary research, it is a work of the imagination in every sense of that word. Its chief difference from other accounts of "the matter of Britain" is its narrative focus: here is the story of Arthur, of Gwenhwyfar's and Lancelet's illicit love, of the knights who take their places at the great Round Table, of the quests for the Holy Grail, of Mordred's treachery, and all the rest told from a point of view sympathetic to the feminine characters. In his collection of myths and legends, Thomas Bulfinch notes that, if one wants to learn of battles and dates, one should read histories if, in contrast, one wants to learn of a people's culture, of their values and ways of life, one must turn to their literature.

His statement is rendered profoundly true by MZB's most ambitious fantasy: following the relatively familiar events of Arthurian legend from the point of view of the women-- especially of Morgaine of the Fairies--the reader will experience a "shock of recognition" that "this isn't just another version; this is the truth." (7) The "shock" will not be shocking, for it comes as the result of reading farther and farther into a heroic but ordinary world, the "women's world," until one notices the "solidity" of almost everything in the narrative. Following Bulfinch's suggestions, we see The Mists of Avalon not as chronicling of battles and heroic acts but as working out of fated, yet for the most part day-to-day, human relationships.

One of the more notable achievements of this long narrative is the consistently formal yet readable language. Unlike T. H. White's The Once and Future King, which begins

94

by introducing Arthur by the nickname "Wart," MZB's work from its very first sentences employs a language that is appropriate for high fantasy. At the very beginning, Morgaine's prologue establishes the elevated tone:

> Now in truth I have come to be wise-woman, and a time may come when these things may need to be known. But in sober truth, I think it is the Christians who will tell the last tale. For ever the world of Fairy drifts further from the world in which the Christ holds sway. I have no quarrel with the Christ, only with his priests, who call the Great Goddess a demon and deny that she ever held power in this world. (8)

The elevated style is maintained without any sense of artificiality for the duration of the narrative.

Bradley's knowledge of magic and the results of her research into Celtic and early Christian relgious beliefs and rituals make the story of Arthur more convincing than most retellings of the legend. The chief conflict in MZB's narrative is that between the "religions" of the early inhabitants of the British Isles and of the Roman Christians. It is introduced in the opening sentences, and it remains until the last page: how can the old religion--a way of life that reveres the Mother Goddess in all her manifestations--withstand the pressures of a Christianity that is inflexibly opposed to any forms or objects of reverence other than its own? Viviane, Lady of the Lake; Morgaine, her foster-daughter and successor; and the Merlins all are willing to see in the worship of the Christian God the worship of an aspect of the divinity they revere, but the Christians look upon the old religion as false and pagan. The centrality of Morgaine and the involvement of Arthur in this conflict make it possible for The Mists of Avalon to require 876 pages for its telling and yet not be overlong.

As MZB's narrative unfolds, one realizes that the differences between it and other Arthurian retellings depend greatly on character as well as the generally feminine viewpoint. Morgaine, as is conventional, is Arthur's half-sister, but she is not his enemy except in the sense that she must oppose his allegiance to Gwenhwyfar's narrow Christian beliefs. In one sense, MZB does what Malory perhaps should have done, since Malory states that of Arthur's "enemies," only Morgaine was undefeated: she gives Morgaine far more attention. In another, she improves on almost every other rendering of Arthur's character, for in _Mists_ Arthur is an affectionate, sympathetic, bumbling puppy-dog, yet a King. While his better knights can outfight him, they respect his genius for strategy; above all, they respond to his open sincerity with love and absolute loyalty. He is neither the jealous, avenging husband, nor the kind of man who would seek the bed of his aunt. The incest which, according to most accounts, brings about his ruin is a part of the pagan ritual--the "Marriage to the Earth"--that is necessary if he is to become the high king of _all_ Britain.

In her rendering of the old Britain as well as of the new (or Christian one), MZB recreates the traumatic impact of Christianity upon the pagans who inhabited the British Isles, makes the prominence of Arthur--as opposed to other nearly contemporaneous kings--understandable, and gives Morgaine a central role to play. When she was eleven or so, Morgaine was taken by Viviane to be trained as a priestess on the magic isle of Avalon. Viviane knew well what she was about, though she kept the details of her plan to herself, when she trained Morgaine in the old religion of the Mother and in practice kept Morgaine a virgin until the proper time. For Viviane, Morgaine's and Arthur's bloodlines, brought together in a son, would set up a dynasty that, claiming secular allegiance of _every_ soul in England, would free the Druids and other pagans from Christian rule.

Thus, when Arthur was enacting the ritual stag hunt, after which he was to consummate his relation with the Goddess by the sexual act, he was ensuring only that the Old Peoples of Britain would give him their allegiance when he took the throne. He knew he would bed a priestess; Morgaine knew she would yield her maidenhead to the new king. Only after the ritual consummation, and after a second act of lovemaking between "the man and the woman," not "the God and the Goddess" who had preceded them, did they recognize each other in the dawning light.

...She heard his hoarse cry. "Morgaine! You

are Morgaine! Morgaine, my sister! Ah, God, Mary
Virgin, what have we done?"....
     "My brother," she whispered. "Ah, Goddess!
Brother!...."
     But even as she soothed him, despair beat at
her.
     Why did you do this to us? Great Mother,
Lady, why?
     And she did not know whether she was calling
to Viviane, or to the Goddess.

Depicted here as unknowing victims to another's machina-
tions, Arthur and Morgaine both become the characters of
tragedy that few other tellings of Arthurian legend reveal.
     Even Mordred, not merely a bastard begotten by a weak
or lusting Arthur upon his aunt Morgause but instead the
fated son of the High King of Britain and a royal-blooded
priestess of Avalon, is redeemed somewhat: he was bred for
the throne and he knows it. With MZB's refrain--"What of
the King Stag when the young stag is grown?"--echoing
through the latter parts of the narrative, the reader sees
Mordred both as victim and villain. Like both his parents,
he must live the role that was created for him even before
he was conceived.
     And so it is with almost every character in the book,
even Gwenhwyfar. Since the viewpoint character is Morgaine,
one does not expect Arthur's queen to be treated sympathetically, and she is not--at least in the beginning. Her first
appearance is an intrusion: somehow she wanders through the
mists veiling Avalon from Glastonbury to interrupt what may
have been the beginning of a satisfying love between the
virgin Morgaine and her kinsman Lancelet. That she wanders
away from the Christian convent is, of course, significant;
so is Lancelet's solicitude as he and Morgaine return the
frightened child to her proper world.
     With hindsight, however, one realizes what it must have
been like to have been married to the High King knowing that
his choice had been determined by the value of her dowry.
Did Arthur truly want Gwenhwyfar, or was she a burden laid
on him in exchange for a hundred armed horsemen? She really
did not know, for Arthur's immediate declaration of love for
her seemed premature; she could not know that the young king

was utterly without guile, that of course he loved her because she was his wife. Nor do we realize, until MZB reveals it, that Gwenhwyfar's timidity and even her fervent Christian faith are grounded in her literal nearsightedness: outdoors she saw mostly frightening blurs and sought refuge inside walls. Her truly happiest years were spent in the convent where she was educated because, when she was indoors, all things were nearer to her--more visible--and, if she could not see with clarity, she had only to fall back on memory and ritual for comfort.

The emphasis MZB places on the cultural and religious upheaval during Arthur's reign is more important than any single character or incident of plot. Thematically, the book is biased; but then, Morgaine herself reminds us with the first few sentences that she fears the Christians "will tell the last tale," and, until we read her "truth," the Matter of Britain has been, for the most part, a Christian story. What The Mists of Avalon effects is the adoption of a different viewpoint, one that can permit the Christ to have been educated by the Druids and then return to preach among the Jews. This different viewpoint is not wholly feminine, despite the domination of the tale by women characters; it is simply other with respect to what is generally known as Western (European) civilization. MZB postulates and then puts into words a compilation of Celtic truth and mores later overrun by Christianity.

How much of Morgaine's (or MZB's) "truth" is fact we cannot know, for there are "mists" and "veils" of culture through which we cannot see with any clarity. It is probably a fact that what we call Atlantis sank, just as the Biblical Great Flood was very likely related to the same cause: the ice-age glaciers melted and receded, and there came to be a Mediterranean Sea. There were (and are) Druids. Were it not for the Moslem holy wars of conversion, the spread of Christianity throughout "barbarian" Europe would seem more like an imposition and displacement of native values than it does. And somehow, it would seem, before humanity related the acts of copulation and reproduction, the world's religions--not yet formalized, perhaps-- would worship the Great Mother, the Life Giver. (9) Whatever the facts, The Mists of Avalon is powerful enough to create its own truth. The prose style is fit for high fantasy, and the domination of Britain by the Christians is analogous to the arrival of the Age of Man in Tolkien's trilogy.

When she presents the Alfar in The House Between the Worlds, readers accept their existence because the work is fantasy. The Mists of Avalon, however, requires that MZB combine the powerful elements of fantasy with the sturdy factuality of the historical novel and, indeed, of history as well. Much of the Matter of Britain is legend. And the legend arises from at least a few facts and much belief. Ambrosius, Uther Pendragon, waves of Saxon invaders, Taliesin, and a warrior called Arturus are real because they are "believed in." For many, there "was" a High King who oversaw the British kings' various efforts to repel the Saxon invasions; and there was a time when Christianity finally toppled the British peoples' other religious beliefs. The Mists of Avalon can be high fantasy only because MZB succeeds at bringing several worlds or planes together convincingly.

There is Britain, simply a locality in our own world, and MZB takes its temporal predecessor to be the main setting for her work. There are records of the Druids, and of ancient religions that revered the Mother Goddess, and MZB takes these--and what can be learned about them from the beliefs of contemporary neopagans--to be the models for the religion that gives the isle of Avalon its mystery. And then there are the Alfar--so called farther north than Britain--or the fairy or "little people" as they are known even today. MZB makes them real by introducing mention of them in the first sentences of Mists, yet preserves their credibility by hiding them from prosaic observation.

How, exactly, The Mists of Avalon is made to function simultaneously as high fantasy and historical novel probably cannot be explained in objective, rational terms. The idea that several worlds can occupy the same geographical place is explained and illustrated in The House Between the Worlds. Because such an idea is practically incredible to the contemporary mind--and to some characters in House--the explanation is acceptable only as part of the book itself. The temporal setting of Mists, however, is one during which belief in the supernatural is more ordinary than disbelief, so that any explanation of the geographical coincidence of

Fairy, Avalon, and Glastonbury would intrude upon and disrupt MZB's treatment of the Arthurian legend.

Thus, the quotation from Malory--"...Morgan le Fay was not married, but put to school in a nunnery, where she became a great mistress of magic"--is placed before the acknowledgments, immediately after the copyright page. There, it alerts us to the tenor of the entire book: that Morgaine and magic are essential to the narrative. Then, following the acknowledgments, in the first sentences of _Mists_ itself, Morgaine tells us that the "world of Fairy" is drifting ever farther from the world of ordinary people.

On the page following, Morgaine admits and then authoritatively dismisses the possibility of disbelief:

> As I tell this tale I will speak at times of things which befell when I was too young to understand them, or of things which befell when I was not by; and my hearer will draw away, perhaps, and say: This is her magic. But I have always held the gift of the Sight, and of looking within the minds of men and women; and in all this time I have been close to all of them. And so, at times, all that they thought was known to me in one way or another. And so I will tell this tale.

From this point on, it is up to the readers: they may dismiss as the narrator's delusions anything they find that does not fit their own standards of "reality" (and, doing this, distort the narrative itself), or they may accept the terms Morgaine sets forth and enter the "world" created by a work of literature.

Because the study of religions--especially Celtic ones--has been for Bradley a lifetime pursuit, the treatment of the isle of Avalon, the world of Fairy that hides behind it, the sojourns of Morgaine among the little folk, and even the use of herbs and simples by the women of Arthur's court rarely if ever strain readers' credulity. The wealth of detail makes each facet of the narrative equally "realistic," and so we follow our imaginations into a place--a place like "Camelot" which, though legendary, our minds make real--that Marion Zimmer Bradley has been creating, actually, from the time she was a girl of ten. We follow our imaginations, find them enriched, and are content.

1. Private correspondence, August 1979.
2. Web of Darkness had been scheduled for 1983 publication but was postponed until 1984. My commentary here is
based on an almost fully copy-edited manuscript, graciously
provided by David Hartwell, past editor at Pocket Books, and
with the permission of Bradley.
3. The full dedication--in both editions following the
copyright page--reads: "To Poul Anderson, fantasy writer
extraordinary, poet, and translator of Norse epics, for
sharing with me several of his favorite legends, and introducing me to the Alfar--not to mention for informing me that
they were in the common domain, belonging not to any one
writer but to the Commonwealth of Literature. In homage and
admiration."
4. The Dreamstone (New York: DAW Books, 1983).
Cherryh appends an "Afterword" to the narrative; it begins
by explaining that "Ealdwood is a place in faery and has
like all such places an indefinite geography" and concludes
with a guide to the pronunciation and meaning of real Old
English, Welsh, and Celtic names.
5. It is noteworthy that Margaret St. Clair's 1969
novel, The Shadow People, is also set--with much the same
effect of verisimilitude as MZB achieves--in Berkeley and
that its chief character, like Fenton, travels between the
"midworld" (our "real world" and an underground "world" that
is not that of the Alfar nor of the ironfolk but certainly
must be located in the same universe or set of planes.
6. Wolves howl to communicate with one another when
the members of a pack are separated; before a hunt, the pack
usually assembles and howls in chorus--not a human one, but
a ritual nevertheless.
7. Bulfinch's statement appears after the mythology
proper and just before his retelling of European legends.
"Shock of recognition" is the phrase Herman Melville used,
writing about Nathaniel Hawthorne in the review-article
"Hawthorne and His Mosses," to describe the experience of

finding oneself in contact--through the medium of a work of literature--with the genius that effects great imaginative results.

8.   From the "Prologue," The Mists of Avalon (New York: Alfred A. Knopf, Inc., 1983), p. ix. All other quotations are from this text.

9.   Whether or not the first human beings attributed female-ness to the deity they felt was the Life Giver we cannot know. Nevertheless, when asked which were the most significant discoveries of humankind, Margaret Mead said, after mentioning the discovery of fire for cooking, "the secret of paternity." (Public lecture at Lehigh University, Bethlehem, PA, May 1975.) Moreover, it seems that the pre-eminence of the masculine deity is related to the rise of cities, a phenomenon quite late in our species' evolutionary life.

VI. ANNOTATED PRIMARY BIBLIOGRAPHY

A. STORIES

A1 "Another Rib." Fantasy and Science Fiction, June
1963, pp. 112-27. With Juanita W. Coulson as "John J.
Wells." After the destruction of the solar system, the
eighteen men who are the first to reach the planet of another star seem destined to be the last human beings ever.
But people of two sexes, says the friendly alien, are hormo-
nally quite similar. The commander's homophobic fears are
finally laid to rest, yet the human race has a future, after
all.

A2 "Bird of Prey." Venture Science Fiction, May 1957,
pp. 92-120. (Later expanded to be The Door Through Space;
see B8.)

A3 "Black & White." Amazing, Nov. 1962, pp. 76-85. A
black priest and a white woman survive a nuclear holocaust,
face the complexities posed by his race, his vowed celibacy,
his and her love, and a white would-be rapist.

A4 "Blood Will Tell." In The Keeper's Price and Other
Stories. New York: DAW, 1980, pp. 181-96 (see B21). Lew
Alton and Dio Ridenow begin a relationship on Vainwal which
will prove crucial in The Sword of Aldones and Sharra's
Exile.

A5 "The Blue Strangers." 1965 or later; see A11 below.

A6 "Centaurus Changeling." Fantasy and Science Fiction,
April 1954, pp. 85-123. Human doctors say childbirth is
impossible on Theta Centaurus IV, but the protagonist follows the advice and example of the native women. She and
her child become the real ambassadors.

A7 "The Climbing Wave." Fantasy and Science Fiction,
Feb. 1955, pp. 3-55. The descendants of the first interstellar flight return to Earth, expecting a world-state run
smoothly by what technology should have become. Instead,
they find a rural world of villages and artisans with no
desire to leave Earth. They also discover why the possible

"advances" in technology have not become cultural impera-
tives.

A8   "Collector's Item." <u>Satellite</u> <u>Science</u> <u>Fiction</u>, June
1958, pp. 118-27.   By means of a box-top offer and then
trading with other kids, the young protagonist maneuvers the
Space Agency around a Moon Treaty not very different from
the one that actually came to be.

A9   "Conquering Hero." <u>Fantastic</u>, Oct. 1959, pp. 47-76.
A young man is a telepath and empath, and is driven to
repressive amnesia about those times he leaves his isolated
home and "senses" too many strangers, but he's nearly an
adult and cannot stay home forever.

A10   "The Crime Therapist." <u>Future</u> <u>Science</u> <u>Fiction</u>, Oct.
1954, pp. 93-100.   At a time when crime is not quite ex-
tinct, a man who really wants to kill his wife and who
cannot be cured of his psychosis by human means seeks il-
legal "drastic therapy" from a Rigellian doctor.   The off-
worlder's therapy is quite effective.

A11   "Danger: Martian at Large." 1965 or later. (Neither
this nor A5 seen.   According to Bradley, A5 appeared in a
Canadian newspaper; Roger Elwood bought A11 but apparently
never published it.)

A12   "The Day of the Butterflies." <u>The</u> <u>DAW</u> <u>Science</u> <u>Fic-</u>
<u>tion</u> <u>Reader</u>.   Ed. Donald A. Wollheim.   New York: DAW Books,
1976, pp. 183-94.   A young woman lives and works in New York
City, her life bounded by her retyping property deeds,
walking to the subway, and enduring the crush of rush-hour
subway rides.   One day, however, she glimpses another
world—with butterflies, and grass, and parklike environs—
and the glimpses become recurring visions, and the visions
prompt her to ask "what's <u>real</u>?"

A13   "Death Between the Stars." <u>Fantastic</u> <u>Universe</u>, Mar.
1956, pp. 70-83.   A Terran woman defies xenophobic bigotry
to share a starship cabin with a dying nonhuman telepath,
and discovers herself rewarded beyond all human imagining.

A14   "A Dozen of Everything." <u>Fantastic</u>, April 1959, pp.
68-71.   A young woman, about to be married and needing just
about everything to outfit herself as bride, wife, homemaker, etc., discovers that her crazy aunt's gift of a
bottle of "Djinn" can fulfill her every need—and then some!

A15   "Elbow Room." In <u>Stellar</u> <u>Science</u> <u>Fiction</u> <u>Stories</u> <u>#5</u>.
Ed. Judy-Lynn del Rey.   New York: Ballantine Books, 1980

(paper), pp. 124-44. An interior monologue by a "wholly self-reliant" Programmer of isolated Checkout Station, about life in an artificial environment and about the entirely voluntary contact she has with the other personalities with whom she shares her life-space.

A16 "The Engine." Viva, March 1977, pp. 63, 108-10. An account of what happens when the hardware in a women's health spa is refined so that a "workout" can fulfill a woman's every need.

A17 "Exiles of Tomorrow." Fantastic Universe, March 1955, pp. 117-22. In the 26th century, there need be no capital punishment: an unruly individualist would be sent back to the American frontier, a religious fanatic to the Dark Ages. This is the narration of one person who bought reprieve--by going into the past to enforce a law of the future: "It isn't lawful for children to be born before their parents."

A18 "A Genuine Old Master." Galileo Magazine of Science and Fiction, No. 5, (Oct. 1977), pp. 24-29. Two mutated humans from the far future visit a penniless illustrator who, they say, is an "old master." He paints the portrait of one. They are horrified by his accurate rendering of her mutated form, and he has to sell the portrait to a new science-fiction magazine.

A19 "The Hawk-Master's Son." In The Keeper's Price and Other Stories. New York: DAW, 1980, pp. 140-55 (see B21). Originating in a scene in The Heritage of Hastur, the narrative explanation of Kennard Alton's cynical character: his loveless, childless marriage to Caitlin; his humane reasons for living apart from her and marrying Elaine, the Terran woman who bore him Lew and Marius; and, perhaps most important, his early and continuing relationship with Dyan Ardais.

A20 "Hero's Moon." Fantasy and Science Fiction, Oct. 1976, pp. 79-98. When stationed in a dangerous outpost, one observes the rules--or courts instant death. The older character, waiting for his son's graduation and first duty assignment, seems rule-bound. The younger one puts human mercy before the rules. Unfortunately, mercy has no survival value in a hostile environment nor in a bureaucracy.

A21 "The Incompetent Magician." In Greyhaven, An Anthology of Fantasy. New York: DAW, 1983, pp. 137-59 (see

B15). Lythande the Magician, also the protagonist of "The Secret of the Blue Star" (see A33), performs a witchcraft for a stuttering sorcerer who lost his potent wand. In the course of the magicks, Lythande's first love is discovered, ensorceled in a lute, is faced, is freed: and Lythande wonders which magician is "incompetent."

A22 "Jackie Sees a Star." Fantastic Universe, Sept. 1954, pp. 97-101. Radiation from the Big Bombing allows young boy telepathic contact with aliens approaching Earth, and soon there's no doubt that his new friend is not an "imaginary playmate."

A23 "The Keeper's Price." In The Keeper's Price and Other Stories. New York: DAW, 1980, pp. 126-38 (see B21). With Lisa Waters. The story of Hilary Castamir, sixteen-years old and five years in training to be Keeper of Arilinn, who is physically and psychically incapacitated by the forty-day cycles of her womanhood. The story also of Callista Lanart, new to Tower training and still a girl; at the urging of Leonie Hastur, she chooses to delay puberty indefinitely so that she may be a Keeper without enduring the agonies Hilary must.

A24 "Keyhole." Vortex, 1, No. 20 (1953), pp. 123-32. A woman from the future, remembering an event that will occur in the "future" of this story, travels a bit farther back in time to alter the "past" to preserve her own "present."

A25 "The Legend of Lady Bruna." In Legends of Hastur and Cassilda. Berkeley CA: Thendara House, 1979, pp. 6-9 (see B22 and Appendix D). When her brother--an early Lord Alton-is killed, Lady Bruna "marries" his widow as freemate and even becomes Commander of the Guard (hereditary post of the Alton Lord) to ensure that the legitimate Alton heir will not be displaced.

A26 "The Lesson of the Inn." In Sword of Chaos. New York: DAW, 1982, pp. 173-86 (see B37). Originally published in June 1978 in the Darkover fanzine Starstone (no. 2). Hilary Castamir leaves Arilinn Tower, miserable that she will never be a Keeper. At an inn on her way home she learns of others' simple kindness and re-discovers her own.

A27 "Measureless to Man." Amazing, Dec. 1962, pp. 74-107. (Later reprinted as "The Dark Intruder"; see B8.) Earthman on Mars discovers ancient intelligent race living in bodies of lower native life forms near extinction, must decide the fates of the Martians and of the Earthborn chimpanzees in his lab.

A28 "Naughty Venusianne." Caper, Dec. 1956, pp. 16-17, 21. As Spencer Strong and Morgan Ives, pseud. (With Forrest J Ackerman.) Among the mixed company of passengers on an interplanetary spaceship, a young woman is so flirtatious that her husband determines to spank her publicly; the joke turns on him as the null-gravity environment thwarts and distorts his every move.

A29 "Oathbreaker." In Darkover Grand Council VII Program Book. Ed. Ivo Dominguez, Jr. Wilmington DE: The Friends of Darkover, 1984, pp. 5-22. At 19, Dyan Ardais leaves his training at Arilinn Tower after taking the monitor's Oath ("to enter no mind save to help or heal") because his father has murdered his step-mother in a drunken, insane rage. Dyan forces Dom Kyril's will in order to free the Domain of the madman's rule but, by using his laran so, exiles himself forever from all who obey the Towers' laws.

A30 "Peace in the Wilderness." Fantastic Universe, July 1956, pp. 55-79. A newspaper editor must consider means and ends when he learns the truth about the Night Police, Earth United, and a years-long war against invading aliens.

A31 "Phoenix." Amazing, Feb. 1963, pp. 88-97. With Ted White. A young man discovers his latent psi powers when he falls onto his bed after having floated near the ceiling. His discovery includes the ability to know--and therefore control--the nature of things even at the sub-atomic level.

A32 "The Planet Savers." Amazing, Nov. 1958, pp. 83-155. (Later expanded; see B25.) A Terran physician, raised by the Trailmen but with no memory of them because of a severe mental block, may be able to prevent the "Trailmen's disease" from becoming pandemic on Darkover. But first he has to reconcile the two "personalities" he has become.

A33 "The Secret of the Blue Star." In Thieves' World. Ed. Robert L. Asprin. New York: Ace Books, 1979 (paper), pp. 267-94. Adepts of the Blue Star have magical powers only so long as each keeps one great personal secret inviolate. A magician who lost three fingers to Lythande in a fight tries vengefully to discover Lythande's secret by using an almost foolproof spell. Lythande must find a counterspell or no longer be an adept. Set in the same world as "The Incompetent Magician" (A21).

A34 "Somebody Else's Magic." _Fantasy_ and Science Fiction, Oct. 1984 (35th Anniversary Issue), pp. 101-35. Another tale of Lythande (see A21, A33, and Appendix D). The
Adept performs an act of mercy at an unknown woman's death
and thereby falls under the power of the dead woman's sword.
It compels Lythande to return it to a shrine from which men
are barred, and so Lythande's own secret and self come into
mortal danger.

A35 "The Stars are Waiting." _Saturn Magazine of Science
Fiction and Fantasy_, Mar. 1958, pp. 84-94. India, then
Norway, close their borders to all foreigners--suddenly,
mysteriously. An American agent in India stayed behind, to
witness the health and prosperity of all. He is sent to
Washington--no one knows how--and speaks for those who sent
him: "The stars are waiting," but there is no war in space.
Only those who demilitarize completely may join the Commonwealth of the Stars.

A36 "A Sword of Chaos." In _Sword of Chaos_. New York:
DAW, pp. 84-103 (see B37). During the Ages of Chaos, Mhari
Delleray alone survives the siege of Sain Scarp and vows to
avenge her family. She takes from the chapel a sword whose
blade is inscribed "draw me never, save when I may drink
blood"; she turns the sword on her captors, she is avenged,
but the sword is not sated.

A37 "Thendara House." In _Tales of the Free Amazons_.
Berkeley, CA: Thendara House, 1980, pp. 63-72 (see B38).
After the end of _The Shattered Chain_: Magda Lorn's initial
experiences in the Thendara Guild House of the Free Amazons.
Earlier form of chapter in _Thendara House_, B39.

A38 "To Err is Inhuman." _Science Fiction Stories_, Sept.
1959, pp. 30-44. To one human race, infallibility is merely
natural. To attack the Earth-humans is unthinkable, therefore, after Intelligence missions bring back written accounts of space wars won and B.E.M.'s (depicted clearly on
the covers of these documents) soundly defeated.

A39 "To Keep the Oath." In _The Bloody Sun_. Rev. ed.
New York: Ace Books, 1979, pp. 373-408 (see B2). Kindra
(of _The Shattered Chain_) breaks the letter of her oath to
save another woman's life: the story of how Camilla becomes
a Free Amazon.

A40 "The Waterfall." In _The Planet Savers_. New York:
DAW, 1976, pp. 103-16. Sybil, foster-sister to Rohana Ar-

dais, is refused Tower-training by a leronis who senses power but also "something other than laran" in her; Sybil discovers her Gift as amorous Guardsmen die at her whim.

A41 "The Wild One." The Book of Weird Tales #1. (1960), pp. 104-16. In their secluded mountain home, a young husband learns that his wife is a "wildcat." Now, he's heard of werewolves and similar legends, but he cannot determine if or how his wife is changing.

A42 "The Wind People." IF: Worlds of Science Fiction, Feb. 1959, pp. 14-27. Medical officer of starship bears a child by one of an alien world's ephemeral "humans," remains there so that the infant may live. Plays on "sons of God / daughters of men" in Genesis.

A43 "Women Only." Vortex, 1, No. 20 (1953), pp. 26-30. A child is born and its father is dismissed. The interreactions of the new mother and the other women raise a question about "humanity" and answer another about the future of two human sexes.

A44 "Year of the Big Thaw." Fantastic Universe, May 1954, pp. 110-16. A monologue, in dialect, by the Yankee father of a son not born on Earth: "first contact" as it might have happened among nineteenth-century rural folk who mind their own business.

B. NOVELS, COLLECTIONS, AND EDITED ANTHOLOGIES

B1 The Bloody Sun. New York: Ace Books, 1964 (paper). For Bradley, the central work about Darkover. Jeff Kerwin, citizen of Terra, discovers his true home in a tower circle; readers discover the traditions of Darkover and the influence of the Terran Empire.

B2 The Bloody Sun. Rev. ed. New York: Ace Books, 1979 (paper). Restores material deleted from the 1964 edition (and reprints thereof), adds several new chapters, and by referring to characters in Darkover novels written after 1964 provides an integrated vision of the last days of Darkovan tower-technology and Comyn rule.

B3 The Brass Dragon. New York: Ace Books, 1969 (paper). A double: published with Ipomoea by John Rackham. Barry Cowan regains consciousness in a hospital in Texas; what little he can recall is more than a year past, and in California. When his real father finds him and brings him home, Barry not only learns what his brass dragon is but finds himself in an extra-terrestrial conflict. A "flying saucer" story: not original in concept, but well executed.

B4 <u>Children</u> <u>of</u> <u>Hastur</u>. Garden City, NY: Nelson Doubleday, Inc., 1983. Science Fiction Book Club edition of <u>The Heritage</u> <u>of</u> <u>Hastur</u> (B17) and <u>Sharra's</u> <u>Exile</u> (B28), bound together in a hardcover reprint of these DAW novels.

B5 <u>City</u> <u>of</u> <u>Sorcery</u>. New York: DAW Books, 1984 (paper). Concludes the "trilogy" about Darkovan Renunciates of which Jaelle n'ha Melora is the central character, following <u>The Shattered</u> <u>Chain</u> (B29) and <u>Thendara</u> <u>House</u> (B39). All major—and most minor—characters are women. Decidedly a "quest narrative," it brings together women of the Terran Empire, the Thendara Guild House, the Forbidden Tower, and even "the Dark Sisterhood." But the latter years of Camilla's and Magda's lives are left unrecounted and may therefore be material for yet another novel.

B6 <u>The</u> <u>Colors</u> <u>of</u> <u>Space</u>. Derby, CT: Monarch Books, 1963 (paper). Cover art inaccurately suggests juvenile fiction. Human man undergoes permanent surgery to learn firsthand the secrets of interstellar travel kept from humans by a self-styled superior alien race. When his strategem is discovered, his heroism cures the aliens of their racial bigotry.

B7 <u>The</u> <u>Colors</u> <u>of</u> <u>Space</u>. Rev. ed. Norfolk, VA: Donning/Starblaze, 1983 (paper) and New York: Pocket Books, 1983 (paper). One-third longer than the original, this edition restores material deleted from the 1963 edition. The improvement is noticeable, but the illustrations in the Donning edition were apparently chosen with a juvenile audience in mind.

B8 <u>The</u> <u>Dark</u> <u>Intruder</u> <u>and</u> <u>Other</u> <u>Stories</u>. New York: Ace Books, 1964 (paper). A double: published with Bradley's <u>Falcons</u> <u>of</u> <u>Narabedla</u> (B13). With author's "Introduction," collects "The Dark Intruder" (originally published as "Measureless to Man"), "Jackie Sees a Star," "Exiles of Tomorrow," "Death Between the Stars," "The Crime Therapist," "The Stars Are Waiting," and "Black and White."

B9 <u>Darkover</u> <u>Landfall</u>. New York: DAW Books, 1972 (paper). How people from Earth first came to Darkover, first contact with the native <u>Chieri</u>, and how adaptation to Darkover affected the mores of even the first human "Darkovans."

B10 <u>The Door Through Space</u>. New York: Ace Books, 1961 (paper). A double: published with <u>Rendezvous on a Lost World</u> by A. Bertram Chandler. On the planet Wolf--which is uncomfortably like the Dry Towns of Darkover--a man sets out to solve a mystery. It involves teleportation and the use of deadly mechanical birds which are locked onto their victims' unique psi-patterns.

B11 <u>Endless Universe</u>. New York: Ace Books, 1979 (paper). Revision of <u>Endless Voyage</u> (B12); integrates two new novella-length parts with the original narrative, and is thus about twice the length of the 1975 version of the novel.

B12 <u>Endless Voyage</u>. New York: Ace Books, 1975 (paper). Life on a ship which opens new worlds to human colonization: because of time dilation and radiation-induced sterility, crew members become a "family" alienated from the human cultures they serve with their very lives.

B13 <u>Falcons of Narabedla</u>. New York: Ace Books, 1964 (paper). A double; see <u>The Dark Intruder</u> (B8). A young man of the contemporary era, privately experimenting with electromagnetic devices, gets pulled into the far future, into another man's body; after much adventure and clarification of identity, he is welcome in the future world. Contains "Darkovan" elements like a red sun and energy-driven "birds" that are self-guiding missiles.

B14 <u>The Forbidden Tower</u>. New York: DAW Books, 1977 (paper). Sequel to <u>The Spell Sword</u>, (B30), the story of an ex-Keeper's marriage to a Terran, of the intimacies in a telepathic family, and of Damon Ridenow's proof that powerful psionic work need not be confined to the traditional Towers and their archaic conditions.

B15 <u>Greyhaven, An Anthology of Fantasy</u>. New York: DAW Books, 1983 (paper). Edited by Bradley, with her introduction and one of her stories, "The Incompetent Magician" (A21). Works representative of the fantasy and science-fiction "circle" of which Bradley is the most renowned member.

B16 <u>Hawkmistress!</u> New York: DAW Books, 1982 (paper). In the midst of the wars during the Ages of Chaos, Romilly MacAran leaves her family home to mature and to develop her own special _laran_, the "mastery over hawk or horse or hound."

B17 The Heritage of Hastur. New York: DAW Books, 1975 (paper). From alternating narrative viewpoints, tells of the coming of age of Regis Hastur and of Lew Alton's growing involvement in the Sharra Rebellion.

B18 The House Between the Worlds. Garden City, NY: Doubleday, 1980. Set in Berkeley in the relatively near future. What begins as a test of a drug for ESP-enhancement leads Fenton, the protagonist, to actual experiences in other worlds. Notable for the strict adherence to the laws of fantasy ("gates" between the faery world and ours, e.g.) and to extrapolation from contemporary parapsychology.

B19 The House Between the Worlds. Rev. ed. New York: Ballantine (Del Rey) Books, 1981 (paper). Restores material deleted from Doubleday edition (B18), is otherwise revised to be Bradley's definitive version of the novel.

B20 Hunters of the Red Moon. New York: DAW Books, 1973 (paper). (Paul Zimmer wrote the combat scenes; Bradley revised them for the final draft.) An Earthborn adventurer is kidnapped aboard a "flying saucer" and meets intelligent beings evolved from nearly every form of life, including a species who makes him and his friends "Sacred Prey" in a ritual (but for most prey fatal) days-long Hunt.

B21 The Keeper's Price and Other Stories (anthology). New York: DAW Books, 1980. Short fiction about Darkover. Includes three stories by Bradley: "Blood Will Tell" (A4), "The Hawk-Master's Son" (A19), and "The Keeper's Price" (A23).

B22 Legends of Hastur and Cassilda (anthology). Berkeley, CA: Thendara House Publications, 1979 (paper). Includes "The Legend of Lady Bruna" (A25) by Bradley.

B23 The Mists of Avalon. New York: Alfred A. Knopf, 1983. The "Matter of Britain" retold as an original high fantasy grounded in research into legend, chronicle, history, religion, and magic. The chief characters are Morgaine le Fay, Arthur's half-sister, and the other women whose presence give a sense of continuity to the deeds of those who sat at Arthur's Round Table.

B24 Oath of the Renunciates. Garden City, NY: Nelson Doubleday, Inc., 1983. Science Fiction Book Club edition of The Shattered Chain (B29) and Thendara House (B39); hardcover reprint of these DAW novels.

B25 The Planet Savers. New York: Ace Books, 1962 (paper). A double: published with The Sword of Aldones (B36). See A32 for plot; this first "Darkover novel" introduces Regis Hastur, telepath and Comyn Lord, as well as Kyla, the guide who is a Free Amazon.

B26 The Ruins of Isis. Norfolk, VA: Donning/Starblaze, 1978 (paper). An archeologist uses the accident of his wife's having taken his name to gain entry to Isis/Cinderella, a female-supremacist world banned from the Unity because of its sexism. Examination of gender-role expectations and behaviors in a then-"controversial" narrative.

B27 Seven from the Stars. New York: Ace Books, 1962 (paper). A double: published with Worlds of the Imperium by Keith Laumer. Marooned on Earth, knowing that the Rhu'inn have already made inroads on this planet, and faced by disbelief in the existence of human beings from another world, the small group of survivors have to convince some Earthpeople fast--and have to fight against their cosmic enemies at the same time.

B28 Sharra's Exile. New York: DAW Books, 1981 (paper). In Bradley's words, "serious treatment by a matured writer (of the characters and) events in the same time frame as Sword (of Aldones)" (B36).

B29 The Shattered Chain. New York: DAW Books, 1976 (paper). Focuses on the women of Darkover: Lady Rohana Ardais hires mercenary Free Amazons to rescue her kinswoman from the Dry Towns; Magda Lorne of the Terran Empire finds herself agreeing to the Amazon oath; and Jaelle, rescued by Rohana, matures and discovers the cost of being "free."

B30 The Spell Sword. New York: DAW Books, 1974 (paper). Andrew Carr, a Terran on a mapping expedition, is saved by the psychic presence of Callista, Keeper of Arillin kidnapped by the Catfolk. She directs him to Armida, where he meets Damon Ridenow, who is concerned about the disappearance of his kinswoman and the depredations of the Catfolk. The plot is developed and resolved by treating what could be "sword and sorcery" as skill and a proper application of psychology.

B31 Star of Danger. New York: Ace Books, 1965 (paper). Larry Montray at 16 studies all he can about Darkover to prepare for his and his father's relocation. He is mistaken

by Kennard Alton for a Darkovan because of his command of
the language, and the two become friends, each risking his
life for the other in an adventure-filled narrative that
features a scene in the home of a Chieri.

B32 <u>Stormqueen!</u> New York: DAW Books, 1978 (paper). Set
near the beginning of the Ages of Chaos. Dorilys, sole heir
to Aldaran, discovers and puts to use her <u>laran</u>-control of
lightning, Allart Hastur learns some control of his "time-
seeing" <u>laran</u> and accepts the crown for the sake of peace,
and the Towers reconsider their earlier practice of making
<u>laran</u>-weapons without thought of their effect.

B33 <u>Survey Ship</u>. New York: Ace Books, 1980 (paper).
The beginning of a first interstellar exploration: all the
characters are adolescents (so that they may live to complete the voyage), highly intelligent, and multi-skilled.
How these young adults grow up, needing to depend on one
another and on accurate self-knowledge for their survival.
At time of initial contract, a sequel was planned.

B34 <u>The Survivors</u>. New York: DAW Books, 1979 (paper).
(In formal collaboration with Paul Edwin Zimmer.) Sequel to
<u>Hunters of the Red Moon</u>. Disappearance of Unity personnel
on uncivilized planet requires investigation; Dane, Rianna,
and Aratak are the only proven "warriors" in the Unity, so
they get the job.

B35 <u>Sword and Sorceress</u> (anthology). New York: DAW
Books, 1984 (paper). Narratives of heroic fantasy in which
<u>women</u> wizards and warriors predominate. Includes a critical
introduction by Bradley about women's place in "Sword-and
sorcery" fiction. Followed (in 1985) by <u>Sword and Sorceress
II</u> (see C5 and Appendix D).

B36 <u>The Sword of Aldones</u>. New York: Ace Books, 1962
(paper). A double; see <u>The Planet Savers</u> (B25). The Comyn
Council commands Lew Alton to return to Darkover. He does,
bringing with him the awesomely powerful Sharra Matrix,
which renews the conflicts of the Sharra Rebellion. Only
the Sword of Aldones can overpower the forbidden matrix;
Lew, Regis Hastur, and Dio Ridenow use it successfully, but
at great cost.

B37 <u>Sword of Chaos</u> (anthology). New York: DAW Books,
1982 (paper). Short fiction about Darkover. Includes two
stories by Bradley: "The Lesson of the Inn" (A26) and "A
Sword of Chaos" (A36).

114

B38 <u>Tales</u> <u>of</u> <u>the</u> <u>Free</u> Amazons (anthology). Berkeley, CA: Thendara House Publications, 1980 (paper). Short fiction about the Darkovan Free Amazons; includes "Thendara House" (A37) by Bradley.

B39 <u>Thendara</u> <u>House</u>. New York: DAW Books, 1983 (paper). Sequel to <u>The</u> <u>Shattered</u> <u>Chain</u> (B29). Magda's experience as a "Free Amazon," Jaelle's experience as the wife of a Terran Empire agent. Much thematic emphasis on a person's conflicting responsibilities (to herself and to those whom she loves), much explanation and interrelation of characters and incidents from several other of the Darkover novels.

B40 <u>Two</u> <u>to</u> <u>Conquer</u>. New York: DAW Books, 1980 (paper). Set toward the end of the Ages of Chaos, during the lifetime of Varzil the Good. Bard di Asturien gets help from his exact double (teleported from Earth by matrix); origin of the Compact; healer-priestesses and mercenary Amazons join, become Renunciates.

B41 <u>Web</u> <u>of</u> <u>Darkness</u>. Norfolk, VA: Donning/Starblaze, 1983; Reprinted, New York: Pocket Books, 1984 (both paper). Although listed in Donning's catalog as a November 1983 publication, this edition was not distributed until early 1984. A much-revised version of the second half of the long fantasy that MZB originally wrote in her teens. Sequel to <u>Web</u> <u>of</u> <u>Light</u> (B42), the story of Deoris (younger sister of Domaris), her love for Riveda (Adept, but not a priest of Light), and the personal relationships of the two sisters and their children. Set on Earth perhaps a decade before the inevitable sinking of Atlantis.

B42 <u>Web</u> <u>of</u> <u>Light</u>. New York: Pocket Books, 1983 (paper) and Norfolk, VA: Donning/Starblaze, 1983 (paper). This listing accurately indicates that the Pocket Books <u>reprint</u> appeared or was distributed before the Donning original. From the same revised manuscript (as B41), the story of Micon and Domaris, their love, and the beginnings of the events that--because of the clash between white and black magics--eventually change the very character of our Earth. Ends with the death rites of fated Micon and the promise embodied in his and Domaris' son, Micail.

B43 <u>The</u> <u>Winds</u> <u>of</u> <u>Darkover</u>. New York: Ace Books, 1970 (paper). A double: published with <u>The</u> <u>Anything</u> <u>Tree</u> by John Rackham. Melitta Storn must seek help, for her crippled brother cannot fight the bandits who capture their home.

Terran Dan Barron finds his mind invaded by Melitta's brother, yet helps Melitta to enlist the aid of Desideria, the
forge-folk, and even the fire-goddess Sharra.
B44 The World Wreckers. New York: Ace Books, 1971
(paper). Absolutely ruthless commercial interests employ an
ecology-imbalancing corporation with the intent of forcing
Darkover into the Terran Empire. Sensing the end of Darkovan autonomy, Regis Hastur sends to every telepath in the
galaxy an invitation to join the kind of experiment that
Darkover can still support. The "world wreckers" amid so
many telepaths can neither conceal their intentions nor
fully attain their ends. The last novel in the Darkovan
"series."

VII. ANNOTATED SECONDARY BIBLIOGRAPHY

The following list of works about Marion Zimmer Bradley's
science fiction is unusual in two respects. First, it is
extremely selective owing to the comprehensive listings
available in C1. Most criticism of Bradley's science fiction exists in the form of very short reviews, brief mentions of her and her work in books of larger scope, and
encyclopedia-style articles; the first are rarely helpful to
the person who wants to know more than generally what to
expect from a specific novel or story, and the last are
superseded by the information provided here, especially in
Chapters 1 and 11. (The author of two of these bio-critical
essays is the author of the present volume; one hopes she
knows more now than she did in 1979, when she wrote them.)
Second, it includes several essays by Bradley herself. Since
these are critical and discursive rather than extensions of
her fiction, they are more appropriately listed here rather
than in the preceding chapter.

C. CRITICISM OF BRADLEY'S WORK(S)

C1 Arbur, Rosemarie. Leigh Brackett, Marion Zimmer Bradley, Anne McCaffrey: A Primary and Secondary Bibliography.
Boston: G. K. Hall & Co., 1982. The middle section is the
definitive bibliography to date, comprising 104 of the 236
pages of bibliographical entries. All entries except those
in "Part A: Fiction" are annotated. Cut-off date for fiction is June 1980 and for miscellaneous media, non-fiction,
and criticism of Bradley's works is April 1980. Chapter VI,
here, supersedes "Part A." The 48-page Introduction addresses the relation among the three authors as well as Bradley's achievements by themselves. Separate indices for
"Works by Bradley" and, listed by author, "Critical Studies
of Bradley." "Introduction" more general than Chapter II

here; overall, a starting place for serious Bradley scholarship.

C2 Bradley, Marion Zimmer. "Darkover Retrospective." Bound with The Planet Savers and The Sword of Aldones reprint. New York: Ace Books, 1980 (paper), pp. 301-59. Long essay that explores the origin of the Darkover story, explains the reasons for the inconsistencies, and examines the lure of the same alien setting; also discusses parallels between her personal interests and those of the author (in the present volume called "MZB") who writes about Darkover.

C3 _____. "An Evolution of Consciousness." Science Fiction Review, No. 22 (Aug. 1977), pp. 34-45. (Although a fanzine, SFR can be found at those libraries that have special science-fiction collections.) Short professional autobiography. Explains publishing standards during the era of the pulp magazines, argues that Pamela Sargent's negative comments about Leigh Brackett (in Women of Wonder) betrays an ignorance of science-fiction history. Discusses two unsalable novels which provided material and ideas for her later published fiction. Notes without false humility the number of SF firsts she has accomplished.

C4 _____. "Experiment Perilous." Experiment Perilous: Three Essays on Science Fiction. New York: Algol Press, 1976 (paper), pp. 7-20. (Shorter version published in Algol, No. 19 (Nov. 1972), pp. 4-11. In either form, as accessible as C3.) About changes in science fiction: the "New Wave," explicit treatment of sex, fuller characterization, and how science fiction has taken up the challenge of dealing with emotional and psychological experiences.

C5 _____. "Introduction: The Heroic Image of Women: Woman as Wizard and Warrior." Sword and Sorceress. Ed. Marion Zimmer Bradley. New York: DAW Books, 1984, pp. 9-13. Essay that describes, analyzes, and evalutates. The nature, process, and function of this now-prevalent variation on (the usually masculine-oriented) "Sword-and-sorcery" fantasy literature.

C6 _____. Introductions to the nine hardcover reprints of Darkover novels. Boston: Gregg Press, 1979. Taken together, enlightening commentary on the novels themselves and matters related to them (influences on the novels, serious psychological research that contributed to their plots, her concept of Darkover as an extended Gedan-

<u>kenexperiment</u> or thought-experiment, and more).

C7 _____. "My Trip Through Science Fiction." <u>Algol</u> 15, No. 1 (Winter 1977), pp. 10-20. (Also a fanzine; same accessibility as C3.) Professional autobiography that complements C3. About <u>The Bloody Sun</u>, which she considers her first adult science-fiction work, her own early sense of alienation (not just a "mere girl" but worse: with brains) and how science fiction alleviated it, affirms that science fiction is a "world" to which she belongs, recounts Anne McCaffrey's gift of Ursula K. Le Guin's <u>The Left Hand of Darkness</u> at a time when her sense of wonder needed it.

C8 Breen, Walter. <u>The Darkover Concordance: A Reader's Guide</u>. Berkeley, CA: Pennyfarthing Press, 1979. Large format (8.5" x 11"), 163 pages, contents arranged alphabetically, with appendices. Very clear, very full treatment of virtually every aspect of the Darkover novels through <u>The Forbidden Tower</u> (1977). Exhaustive, absolutely precise and correct; a necessity for the serious scholar—and the curious fan—interested in the Darkover novels.

C9 _____. <u>The Gemini Problem</u>. Baltimore: T-K Graphics, 1975 (paper; accessibility limited: see C3 or C9 below). Clear and detailed authoritative analysis and explication of Darkover as MZB's favorite setting and of her literary artistry as made evident by the series.

C10 Friends of Darkover. <u>Darkover Newsletter</u>. Bimonthly fanzine devoted to Darkover and other science-fiction universes. Clearing house of information about privately printed Darkover booklets—for example, <u>Costume and Clothing as a Cultural Index</u>...—and how to locate them. (Friends of Darkover / Box 72 / Berkeley, CA 94701; send self-addressed stamped envelope for reply.) Of particular value are items by MZB and comments or short essays by regular fans as well as professionals, including C. J. Cherryh, Randall Garrett, Jacqueline Lichtenberg, Elizabeth A. Lynn, Andre Norton, Baird Searles, Wilmar H. Shiras, and Donald A. Wollheim.

C11 Leith, Linda. "Marion Zimmer Bradley and Darkover." <u>Science-Fiction Studies</u> No. 20 (March 1980), pp. 28-35. Significant because it is the first article to appear in a scholarly journal that is devoted solely to the Darkover novels. Discusses MZB's bringing together of contraries, treatment of individuals' maturation and of sexuality, and literary development. Valuable citations of the debate about <u>Darkover</u> <u>Landfall</u> and its denial of abortion to a character. (These last are also listed in C1, p. 170.)

C12 Lupoff, Richard A. Introduction to <u>The</u> <u>Sword</u> <u>of</u> <u>Aldones</u>. Reprint. Boston: Gregg Press, 1977, pp. v-xx. Authoritative essay on Bradley's development from fan to writer which notes that her preference to be published in paperback has kept her from being considered a "serious" science-fiction author. Notably informative.

C13 Shwartz, Susan M. "Marion Zimmer Bradley's Ethic of Freedom." In <u>The</u> <u>Feminine</u> <u>Eye:</u> <u>Science</u> <u>Fiction</u> <u>and</u> <u>the</u> <u>Women</u> <u>Who</u> <u>Write</u> <u>It</u>. Ed. Tom Staicar. New York: Frederick Ungar, 1982, pp. 73-88. Incisive analysis of MZB's thematic statements about personal freedom in the Darkover novels and stories, especially <u>The</u> <u>Shattered</u> <u>Chain</u>. Explanation of the Darkovan fact that "any attempt at change or progress carries with it the need for pain-filled choice."

C14 Sturgeon, Theodore. Introduction to <u>Darkover</u> <u>Landfall</u>. Reprint. Boston: Gregg Press, 1978, pp. v-viii. High praise for the humanity as well as the expertness with science-fiction requirements and conventions in MZB's work; notes that Bradley was a fan who became a "Big One" (i.e., major science-fiction author).

C15 Wood, Susan. Introduction to <u>The</u> <u>Heritage</u> <u>of</u> <u>Hastur</u>. Reprint. Boston: Gregg Press, 1977, pp. v-xxvi. Clearly feminist perspective. Examines development of the Darkover series and of MZB as a writer; mentions change of science-fiction marketing demands by 1970 and how MZB's fiction responded, with fully developed characters and adult treatment of adult matters, one of which is the cultural status of women.

APPENDICES

APPENDIX A:

PUBLICATION HISTORY OF DARKOVER FICTIONS

The following list gives the date for the first commercial publication of each work, unless the work has been published only by a small press; in the latter case, "(SP)" alerts the reader that the work is very unlikely to be available even in specialty bookstores. Further, "KP" and "SC" here iden-tify the two anthologies, The Keeper's Price and Other Stories and Sword of Chaos, both published by DAW Books. The reader is referred to Chapter VI and to Chapter VII, entry C10, for details of the small-press publication of other stories.

The Planet Savers. Ace, 1962.
The Sword of Aldones. Ace, 1962.
The Bloody Sun. Ace, 1964.
Star of Danger. Ace, 1965.
The Winds of Darkover. Ace, 1970.
The World Wreckers. Ace, 1971.
Darkover Landfall. DAW, 1972.
The Spell Sword. DAW, 1974.
The Heritage of Hastur. DAW, 1975.
The Shattered Chain. DAW, 1976.
"The Waterfall." Ace, 1976.
The Forbidden Tower. DAW, 1977.
Stormqueen!. DAW, 1978.
The Bloody Sun, revised. Ace, 1979.
"To Keep the Oath." Ace, 1979.
"The Legend of Lady Bruna." (SP), 1979.
Two to Conquer. DAW, 1980.
"Blood Will Tell." KP, DAW, 1980.
"The Keeper's Price." KP, DAW, 1980.
"The Hawkmaster's Son." KP, DAW, 1980.
"Thendara House." (SP), 1980.
Sharra's Exile. DAW, 1981.

"The Lesson of the Inn." <u>SC</u>, DAW, 1982.
"A Sword of Chaos." <u>SC</u>, DAW, 1982.
<u>Hawkmistress!</u> DAW, 1982.
<u>Thendara House</u>. DAW, 1983.
<u>City</u> <u>of</u> <u>Sorcery</u>. DAW, 1984.
"Oathbreaker." (SP), 1985.

APPENDIX B:

UNOFFICIAL MAP OF DARKOVER, REGION OF THE DOMAINS

The map below owes much to those printed on the endpapers of
the 1979 Gregg Press reprints of Darkover novels and on the
pages following the dedication page of The Heritage of
Hastur (New York: DAW Books, 1975). In City of Sorcery
(1984) MZB "renovates" the geomorphology of the entire planet: "beyond the Hellers, as far as anyone knew (and now
the Empire knew Cottman Four considerably better than the
Darkovans themselves), was nothing; only the impenetrable
mountain range known as the Wall around the World. And
beyond the Wall, nothing but barren icy wastes stretching
from pole to pole" (p. 25). Thus, this map helps only
minimally to clarify the geographical setting of that novel.
Besides, Bradley has been explicit: "I disclaim any and all
maps of Darkover" (private correspondence, June 1983). Yet
some readers will find this map a general if incomplete
guide, and others may want to use it as a "rough draft" as
they draw their own.

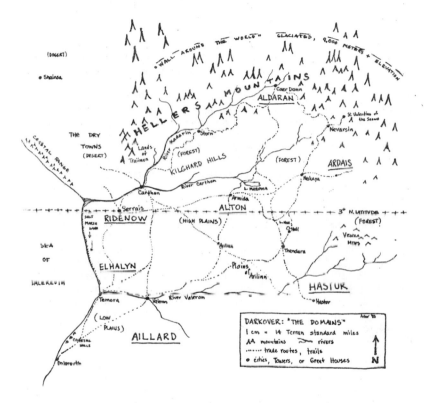

DARKOVER: "THE DOMAINS"
1 cm = 14 Terran standard miles
ᴧᴧ mountains ⌇ rivers
.... trade routes, trails
● cities, Towers, or Great Houses

APPENDIX C:

DARKOVAN PRONUNCIATION, A BEGINNING

The following owes much to Walter Breen's "Guide to Pronunciation of Darkovan Words" (The Darkover Concordance, p.
ix) and to Marion Zimmer Bradley's oral and written advice.

The pronunciation of words in the several Darkovan languages
and dialects is, for a created linguistic system, reasonably
consistent. If the reader has a gift for languages and is
fluent in Spanish and Gaelic or another old Celtic tongue,
the following guide should be fully sufficient. If the
reader lacks these ideal qualities, the best practical way
to learn to pronounce troublesome but frequently encountered
Darkovan words is to enlist a friend who does know Spanish
and let her or him say the words aloud after checking the
following list for peculiarly Darkovan variations. Remem-
beringthat the original human settlers of Darkover had for
the most part Celtic and Hispanic surnames will help, too.
So will knowing that even Bradley herself sometimes "mispro-
nounces" a word in a language she has created. Best of all
is to remember that the Darkovan words are just one (minor)
aspect of the whole that the Darkover novels comprise.
    Generally the penultimate or next-to-last syllable of
a word is the accented or most heavily stressed one; normal
English pronounciation of words like "vacation" and "tomorrow" illustrate the Darkovan norm.
    When an apostrophe appears within a Darkovan word, it
signifies a separation of syllables that are nonetheless
elided or "slurred together"; the separation is similar to
but slightly greater than what happens in English with
"there'd" (for "there would").
    The Darkovan languages, unlike English, have few
diphthongs, or sets of two vowels that indicate a single
sound the way that "straight" (which rhymes with "mate")
does. Darkovans pronounce each vowel separately, as we do

126

when we say "PO em" instead of "POME." Thus "Jaelle" is
pronounced "zhay ELL uh" (J sounds like the S in "measure"
and "treasure"). The most common exceptions to the Darkovan
"one vowel, one sound" rule are listed after the vowels,
below.

VOWELS:

(A)   usually as in "father"
(E)   within a word, as in "get"; when it is final, an "uh"
      sound softer than the last syllable in "umbrella"; when
      it is accented, the same as in "cliche"
(I)   usually as in "hit"; exceptions occur in words like
      Ridenow, which is pronounced "REED'n oh"
(O)   usually as in "go"
(U)   the same sound as in "fool" but not sounded for so long
      a time
(Y)   usually like the English "ee" sound; when followed by
      "N" and "R," like the "short I" in "pin"; an exception
      occurs in the name "Dyan," which sounds like "DAY an"

DIPHTHONGS OR TWO-VOWEL SETS:

(AI) usually very similar to the sound in "file"
(AU) usually the same as the sound in "ouch"
(EE) generally like the last sound in "cliche"
(EW) very similar to the sound in "computer"

CONSONANTS DIFFERENT FROM ENGLISH ONES:

(G)   preceding A, O, and U, a "hard G" as in "get"; but when
      it precedes E and I, a very "soft G" that sounds like
      the S in "measure"
(J)   same sound as the S in "measure" and "treasury"
(LL) usually just a long L sound
(R)   very short Spanish-sounding R: try the Spanish impera-

tive for "look!" which sounds like "MEE duh" but with
very little D sound
(RR) same as the Spanish pronunciation of RR, a rolled R
sound
(TH) same as "thin," not the same as "these"; when at the
end of a word, very nearly a T

THE FAMILY NAMES OF THE DOMAINS:

Aillard	=	"aye LARD"
Aldaran	=	"AHL duh rin"
Alton	=	"AHL tin"
Ardais	=	"ahr DAZE"
Elhalyn	=	"el HAHL in"
Hastur	=	"HAH stir"
Ridenow	=	"REED'n oh"

APPENDIX D: FORTHCOMING WORKS

(Note: this list is based on telephone interviews with Bradley and correspondence with Elisabeth Waters, her secretary. While time may prove it somewhat inaccurate and certainly incomplete, as of 30 December 1984 it is as definitive as possible.)

The Best of Marion Zimmer Bradley. Collection in preparation by Academy Chicago Press. Publication date uncertain.

The Dark Brother. A Darkover novel about twins who are telepaths, inspired by the film, The Corsican Brothers, which featured Douglas Fairbanks, Jr. Publication by DAW Books, likely in late 1986.

The Firebrand. Narrative drawing upon the legends about and the "history" of the Trojan War, told from the perspectives of major feminine characters. A major work; manuscript to Knopf in October 1985 (Ballantine will publish the paperback edition). If other similarities to The Mists of Avalon--publisher and general narrative process are two--publication could occur in 1987, possibly late 1986.

Free Amazons of Darkover. Anthology, with introduction and two stories--"The Legend of Lady Bruna (A25) and "Knives (below)--by Bradley. Publication by DAW Books in mid-1985.

"Knives." In Free Amazons of Darkover (above). The story follows a young woman's coming of age, from her brutal treatment by her step-father to her maturation as a Darkovan "Free Amazon."

Night's Daughter. A legend-and-fantasy novel deriving from the same materials as The Magic Flute: combines fantasy-writing and opera, two of Bradley's long-cherished interests. Publication by Ballantine early in 1985.

"On First Looking Into Bradley's Guidelines." A poem consisting of related limericks by Elizabeth Thompson.

Since it is a versification of the guidelines Bradley
sent to potential contributors to <u>Sword</u> <u>and</u> <u>Sorceress</u>
<u>II</u> (below), it must be considered something of a colla-
boration. In the 1985 anthology mentioned.
"Sea Wrack." The tale of Lythande's encounter with a mermaid. In <u>Moonsinger's</u> <u>Friends</u>, an anthology in tribute
to Andre Norton, edited by Susan Shwartz. Publication
possible in 1985, perhaps 1986.
<u>Sword</u> <u>and</u> <u>Sorceress</u> <u>II</u>. Anthology edited and with an intro-
duction by Bradley. Stories selected according to
their adherence to the guidelines sent to potential
contributors (and a poem that versifies these guidelines). The short introduction is instructive, with
citations of what is <u>not</u> "women's heroic fantasy."
Publication by DAW Books in mid-1985.
"Wandering Lute." A story of Lythande's comical adventures
that follow upon her discovery of a lute that wants to
play with Lythande. To be published in <u>Fantasy</u> <u>and</u>
<u>Science</u> <u>Fiction</u> in late 1985, possible 1986.
<u>Warrior</u> <u>Woman;</u> <u>the</u> <u>Adventures</u> <u>of</u> <u>Zadieyek</u> <u>of</u> <u>Gyre</u>. Novel
about a woman with total amnesia who becomes a gladia-
tor. She is human, but her origin--like the novel's
setting--is a world never before written about by Bradley. Publication by DAW Books in late 1985.
(To lend an appropriate note of uncertainty to this Appen-
dix: "Return to Darkover" and/or <u>Return</u> <u>to</u> <u>Darkover</u> is not
on Marion Zimmer Bradley's current writing schedule.)

INDEX

thematic conflict, 52
Terran Empire, Bradley's sympathies for, 28
Terran-Darkovan cultural conflict, 81
Terran-Darkovan cultural contrast, 52
"That Only a Mother," 78
Thematic comments, 23
Thematic emphasis shifting, 81
Thematic meaning of magic, 81
Thematic use of sex, 81
Theme defined, 71-72
Themes, recurring:
anti-materialism, 71, 82
familial social bonding, 76
intimacy by way of empathy, 77
nature of intimacy, 71
quest for family, 71
tolerance, 71
use of technology, 57
womanhood, 71
Thendara House, 22, 47, 62, 80, 81
Thendara House as sequel, 47
Thendara House dependent on The Shattered Chain, 81
Thendara House, hallucinations, 47
Thendara House, imagery, 47
"Thought-experiment," 27, 41
Threshold sickness, 62
Time-travel, early treatment of, 66
Tiptree, James Jr., 25
"To Keep the Oath," 43, 61
Tolkien, J. R. R., 22, 91, 99
Tower, 48, 58, 59-60, 61
Two to Conquer, 24, 44, 53, 60, 62, 82
Unity, the, 34

Variety in works: causes, 79
Varzil the Good, 24
Verisimilitude, 88
Viewpoint character in The Mists of Avalon, 97
Viviane, 95

"Waterfall, The," 43
We Who Are About to..., 27
Web fantasy, 94
Web novels and fancy, 94
Web of Darkness, 85, 87
Web of Light, 22, 85, 86, 87
Werfel, Franz, 48
White man's superiority in science-fiction, 67
White, T. H., 94
"Wife" as sexist word, 70
Winds of Darkover, 33, 46
Wollheim, Donald A., 33, 40, 42, 79
Wollheim friend, not just editor, 33
Wolves' howling, 93
Woman's viewpoint, value as novelty, 65
"Women Only," 65, 67, 69, 71
Word For World Is Forest, The, 35
Works nominated for major awards, 74
World Wreckers, The, 33, 60, 61, 73, 74
dedication, 33
Worldhouse, 88
Writers are liars, 69
Writing difficulties in the late sixties, 32-33

"Year of the Big Thaw," 69
Zimmer, Paul Edwin (Bradley's brother), 78

LITERATURE

$9.95

The Work
of
Julian May

Julian May burst onto the science fiction world with her classic novelette, "Dune Roller," which created an immediate sensation upon its original publication in 1951, and has since been reprinted in seven different anthologies, as well as being made into a motion picture, teleplay, and radio play. Just as quickly, however, she turned her polytropic talents to other fields, penning an incredible 7,000 encyclopedia articles during the mid-1950s. In 1957, she was approached by Popular Mechanics Press to write a series of popular science books for young people. The success of these publications soon led to other projects for the juvenile book market, including fiction, sports biographies, Americana, popular music, film books, and many others. During a fifteen-year period between 1966-1981, May published some 250 different titles for young people, and was acclaimed by Library Journal, Booklist, Horn Book, and many others for her clear, unencumbered writing style, and for her ability to explain complex notions in terms that children could readily understand. Her first love had always been science fiction, however, and in the late 1970s she began developing a multi-book project called The Saga of Pliocene Exile. Publication of the first novel in this series, The Many-Colored Land, fulfilled the early promise of "Dune Roller," and immediately established her as a major writer of fantastic literature. This is the first published bibliography of her work.

Bibliographies of Modern Authors provide complete, annotated bibliographies of the works of popular or significant writers of the modern era, revised and updated at regular intervals for the most comprehensive and timely coverage available.

☆ **Starmont House** ☆
P.O. Box 851, Mercer Island, Washington 98040, USA

**STARMONT
H O U S E**

P O BOX 851
MERCER ISLAND, WA 98040 U S A
(206) 232-8484

7 books about
Stephen King

Having published the first book-length study of Stephen King (The Reader's Guide to Stephen King, 1982), Starmont House is proud to announce, as the culmination of its in-depth critical studies program, the forthcoming publication of seven volumes on the works and life of Stephen King. Presenting the various aspects of the work of America's most popular writer, we will be publishing, in the months of July through November 1985, in both trade paperback and hardcover form, the following titles:

[1] DISCOVERING STEPHEN KING, edited by Darrell Schweitzer
Prismatic in their effect, here is a selection of 16 essays on Stephen King and his work, presented by an array of writers who have demonstrated their ability to deal with the masterly talent of this literary phenomenon.

[2] STEPHEN KING AS RICHARD BACHMAN, by Michael R. Collings
It was startling news that a previously undisclosed body of work had been published by Stephen King under a pseudonym. This book-length study of his "hidden" works -- The Rage, The Long Walk, The Running Man, Road Work and Thinner -- will be of immense interest to all of his readers.

[3] THE SHORTER WORKS OF STEPHEN KING, by Michael R. Collings and David Engebretson
Besides being a prime novelist, Stephen King is widely noted for his shorter works, both in the short story and novella length. This book covers his entire output to date. Readers will be delighted with the intriguing resumes and analyses in this volume.

[4] THE MANY FACETS OF STEPHEN KING, by Michael R. Collings
Here is a fascinating study of his novels, their various interrelationships and with those of "Richard Bachman." A chronology of all his work, a discussion of King as critic and an overview of his shorter work and films follow. Collings has an informative work here that brings King's readers right up to date on his life and works in progress.

[5] THE STEPHEN KING CONCORDANCE, by David Engebretson
This is a complete concordance to the novels and short fiction of Stephen King, covering key words and phrases, proper names, geographical locations and recurring themes and images. A concordance of this type will be an invaluable aid to King readers and scholars. Various helpful lists are included.

[6] THE FILMS OF STEPHEN KING, by Michael R. Collings

This book will consider the quality of the film versions, both as films and as adaptations of King's narratives. It will incorporate film theory and criticism, reviews and interviews with those responsible for the films, and independent insights gleaned from multiple viewings of the films and readings of the narratives. All past works will be covered in detail, as well as such forthcoming productions as Silver Bullet, The Body, Maximum Overdrive, The Stand, Pet Sematary, The Long Walk and The Running Man. The various television productions will also be covered. A filmography listing all films, including production companies, directors, producers, actors, and other key personnel will be included.

[7] THE STEPHEN KING PHENOMENON, by Michael R. Collings

Stephen King is many things. This volume addresses the many questions relating to King as social phenomenon rather than as literary figure. It will move in two directions: outward from King, and inward toward him. Moving outward, we see King as social critic, not only in his fiction but in his other writings, beginning as early as the "Garbage Truck" columns. Moving inward, we see critics focusing on King as barometer of contemporary society, responding to deep needs in American (and international) readers. This book will consider King from extra-literary perspectives -- not so much what he has written as who he is and how he has changed us.

Trade Paperback -- $9.95 -- Hardcover -- $17.95

Order now for shipment immediately upon publication.

STARMONT HOUSE, INC.
P.O. Box 851
Mercer Island, WA 98040 USA
[206]-232-8484

Please enter our order for the following:

[1] DISCOVERING STEPHEN KING - HC____ PB____
[2] STEPHEN KING AS RICHARD BACHMAN - HC____ PB____
[3] THE SHORTER WORKS OF STEPHEN KING - HC____ PB____
[4] THE MANY FACETS OF STEPHEN KING - HC____ PB____
[5] THE STEPHEN KING CONCORDANCE - HC____ PB____
[6] THE FILMS OF STEPHEN KING - HC____ PB____
[7] THE STEPHEN KING PHENOMENON - HC____ PB____

Enclosed is remittance in the amount of $____./ As library or dealer, bill us [ ].
Name: _____ _____
Address: _____
City: _____ State: _____ Zip: _____